# Praise for I A D1495635

Have you ever felt confused about how a good God can allow the pain in your life? If so, I cannot encourage you enough to read *I Am Strong*. This message will anchor your soul and give flight to your faith. Most importantly, it will draw you closer to the God who wants to heal your hurts.

**Jim Cymbala,** pastor of the Brooklyn Tabernacle
and bestselling author of numerous books, including
*Fresh Wind, Fresh Fire* and *Breakthrough Prayer*

Pain and suffering often drive people away from God. John Dickerson's *I Am Strong* takes a different path. In a counterintuitive way and with deep biblical roots, he shows how we can be strong when we allow pain and suffering to take us to God. The path he recommends does not lead to despair but to hope. In fact, Dickerson takes us to the only hope there is in the midst of the deep pain that life often delivers.

**Dr. Darrell Bock,** *New York Times* bestselling author,
Humboldt Scholar, and senior research professor of New
Testament Studies at Dallas Theological Seminary

To write a book about hope and strength in the midst of suffering requires that one understands both sides of the equation. John S. Dickerson not only has experienced both sides, but with his heart and pen, he has mapped out a practical guide for the journey to light for all who travel down the dark road of pain and suffering. Read it when you need hope the most; share it with a friend in the midst of their trial; and use it in your small groups because *everyone* can benefit from this helpful and sensitive work.

**Chuck Bentley,** CEO of Crown Financial Ministries and author of
*The Worst Financial Mistakes in the Bible and How You Can Avoid Them*

Life has a way of falling apart just when we least expect it. In *I Am Strong*, John S. Dickerson reveals the hidden strength that God provides in our darkest moments and shows how to access it daily. If you're walking through a valley or know someone who is, this is a must-read.

**Larry Osborne,** author of *Thriving in Babylon* and
pastor of North Coast Church, California

John Dickerson is quickly becoming one of my favorite authors. In his new book *I Am Strong*, John digs deep into what it really means to go through difficult times. He then reminds us that God can and will bring good from the struggles and tragedies we face. And while our circumstances may be painful at the moment, we need to remember it's not the end of our story, but simply the beginning of a new chapter.

**Steve Poe,** lead pastor of Northview Church, Carmel, Indiana

Pastor John Dickerson is one of the great writers of our time. His most recent book contains wisdom that has already benefited me, as it will those who read and reflect on its messages.

**Terence F. Moore,** president emeritus of MidMichigan Health System

As a grief counselor and pastor, I minister daily to people who are sick, hurting, or discouraged. This book contains the life-changing hope I wish I could give to every hurting person who comes my way.

**Dan Rydberg,** Care and Outreach pastor at
Cornerstone Church, Prescott, Arizona

As a cancer survivor and hospital CEO, I am all too familiar with the questions, fears, and uncertainties of suffering. This book contains rock-solid hope, not only for patients, their families, and caregivers, but for anyone facing the challenges and questions that suffering brings.

**Jeff Leimgruber,** hospital CEO and Fellow of the
American College of Healthcare Executives

John Dickerson knows how to speak to people's pain. He was there in the small town of Prescott, Arizona, when word came that nineteen young firefighters had just died. He was there that evening when the whole state of Arizona cried themselves to sleep. He brought hope in the middle of a community's pain, and his book *I Am Strong* will bring hope to you in your pain.

**Dr. Tim Kimmel,** author of *Grace Filled Marriage*

*I Am Strong* uniquely combines the insightful mind of a journalist with the compassionate heart of a pastor. The journey in these pages will feed your soul, renew your hope, and restore your life.

**Chip Ingram,** teaching pastor of Living on the Edge, senior pastor of Venture Christian Church, and author of *Finding God When You Need Him Most*

Followers of Jesus cannot escape pain any more than they can escape this fallen world. Seen in the context of the suffering Jesus and the many who have followed him, pain can bring a believer to full maturity and access to the power of Christ. In *I Am Strong*, John S. Dickerson uniquely combines a pastor's theological training, a shepherd's heart to comfort, and a journalist's question asking and storytelling.

**Cal Thomas,** *USA Today* columnist and author of *What Works*

Living on this sin-encrusted planet greets us with regular doses of pain. We rarely need reminders of its nagging reality. But we do quickly lose sight of hope. This compelling, biblically based, practical book reminds each follower of Jesus of the precious hope that often eludes us when the thorns of pain and suffering dig deep. John S. Dickerson writes not from an ivory tower, void of pain, but is, like most who make life's journey, one who is well-acquainted with its sharp edges. Take, read, and regain hope.

**J. Paul Nyquist, PhD,** president of Moody Bible Institute

As a counselor, I see people who struggle daily with the effects and whys of suffering. In *I Am Strong*, John Dickerson methodically walks us through the steps of making sense of something that does not make sense and depositing our pain at the feet of Christ. It is a powerful book of truth and hope.

**Kim Kimberling, PhD,** leader of the Awesome Marriage Movement and author of *7 Secrets to an Awesome Marriage*

Pain is inevitable. And when it comes, it is crucial to have a road map that helps you navigate a way forward. In *I Am Strong*, John Dickerson delivers such a map. John doesn't offer up a naive, cotton-candy view of the Christian life. From his own journey with a rare health condition and a solid biblical understanding, John provides real-life wisdom and hope for those who are hurting.

**Lance Witt,** founder of Replenish Ministries and
former executive pastor at Saddleback Church

John Dickerson is a good man who gave up a promising career in journalism to serve his God. I am not a believer, as he is. I am, however, a believer in his ability to hold readers in his thrall, to tell simple, uplifting human stories, to share his eloquent hopes.

**Ken Auletta,** media critic for *The New Yorker*,
author, and Pulitzer Prize judge

There is no place on this planet where hurting men and women cannot be found. The discouraging part is that most of them have no idea how to obtain freedom and healing from their painful wounds and circumstances. God never meant for us to live disappointing and defeated lives. John S. Dickerson's journalistic research ability and gentle shepherd's heart will take you on an extraordinary journey of healing in a miraculous way.

**Linda Penn,** host of *Today's Living Hope* on
WDCX 99.5 Radio FM (970 and 990 AM), serving
Western New York and Northern Ontario, Canada

# I Am STRONG

## FINDING GOD'S PEACE AND STRENGTH IN LIFE'S DARKEST MOMENTS

### JOHN S. DICKERSON

ZONDERVAN

*I Am Strong*
Copyright © 2016 John S. Dickerson

This title is also available as a Zondervan ebook. Visit www.zondervan.com/ebooks.

Requests for information should be addressed to:
Zondervan, 3900 *Sparks Dr. SE, Grand Rapids, Michigan* 49546

ISBN 978-0-310-34191-8 (softcover)

ISBN 978-0-310-34192-5 (ebook)

Cover design: *Micah Kandros*
Interior design: *Kait Lamphere*

First Printing October 2015 / Printed in the United States of America

"For when I am weak, then I am strong."
*2 Corinthians 12:10*


". . . whose weakness was turned to strength . . ."
*Hebrews 11:34*

# Contents

## Part 5: Carried—*The Pen and Paper*

# Foreword

*You've probably picked up* this book because you or someone you love is experiencing pain. It may be the pain of a loss of some kind, of a betrayal, of failed health, of a shattered relationship, or of the death of someone close to you.

Having comforted thousands of individuals as a pastor for more than thirty years, I have noticed a few common questions we ask in our pain: *Why is God allowing my suffering? Will God heal my hurting?* And if you're anything like me, you've also wondered, *Will I make it through this?*

How you answer these questions in the midst of your pain will shape your view of God, yourself, your life, and eternity. These are among the most important questions you will ever answer, because pain often alters the destiny of our lives for better or for worse.

And so I'm privileged to recommend my good friend John Dickerson as your guide to lead you to fulfilling, healing, and holistic answers. I've read intellectual books about suffering that discuss pain as hypothetical. And I have read comforting books about pain that fail to wrestle with difficult questions. This book, written in the voice of a caring and guiding friend, speaks to both the heart and the mind in a way that allows you to meet and experience the God of all comfort in a personal and powerful way.

*I Am Strong* uniquely combines the insightful mind of a journalist with the compassionate heart of a pastor. The journey in these pages will feed your soul, renew your hope, and restore your life.

May you find life-anchoring hopes. May you find the God who created you and who loves you, the God who longs to heal you, hold you, and ultimately deliver you out of or through all pain and suffering by His grace.

**Chip Ingram,** teaching pastor of Living on the Edge,
senior pastor of Venture Christian Church, and
author of *Finding God When You Need Him Most*

# Prelude

On June 30, 2013, a forest fire ate its way through the Arizona pines around Prescott, Arizona, where I lived. The flames towered more than two hundred feet high, sending up so much smoke that NASA captured photos of the fire from space. The Yarnell Hill fire burned, in places, at more than two thousand degrees Fahrenheit.

Around 4:42 p.m., that fire overtook and killed nineteen wildland firefighters from our small community. They weren't just nineteen firefighters; they were dads, husbands, sons, and brothers. In the days, weeks, and years since, I have walked with surviving families and fire officials through unimaginable grief, turmoil, and pain.

This book presents the hope many of us have learned to build our lives on.

*This book is written as a gift to anyone who is hurting. It's a word of encouragement:*

- in the grief of unexpected tragedy
- in the daily pain of chronic illness
- in the lifelong struggle of making our way through the sharp edges of this broken world

If you know someone who is hurting, this book is written for them. If they're not a reader, you might get them the audio version to listen to, available at Audible.com or Amazon.com.

If you're reading this for yourself, know that I have prayed for you, asking the God of all comfort to encourage you in these pages, to draw near to you. And this I have seen: If you will reach out to Him, you will find that He is also reaching out to you.

Seek Him, and you will find Him.

# Hope for the Suffering

—————

*Street dogs wandered across* the dirt road in Los Algadones, Mexico, just south of the United States border. I was there to write a story for *The Scottsdale Times* newspaper. Everyone else was there for a different reason—to buy hope.

They had driven RVs and pickup trucks from as far as Oklahoma and Indiana, searching for the Mexican doctor in this border town. The Americans brought hopeless conditions—terminal cancer, incurable COPD, and debilitating headaches—to the clinic.

They lined up to pay $1,000 each for injections advertised as stem cells with miraculous healing properties. Injections that could "save your life." But, as the sales pitch went, "the FDA will not approve them in the U.S." So, hopeful, tired, and sick, American retirees had driven thousands of miles. Hard-earned savings in hand, they ventured into Mexico to find the doctor.

In the end, we titled the investigation "Hope Cells." Because hope does *sell*. It's a multibillion-dollar industry. In this case, desperate folks paid to have blood from goats and other animals injected into them. The "doctor" happily took $1,000 every thirty minutes out of the wallets of the vulnerable, the desperate, and the needy.

I hung out in the clinic lobby. Sat next to Bill Thompson, a sixty-two-year-old farmer with COPD lung disease, his John Deere cap covered in Oklahoma dirt from his cornfields. I talked with Gwen Wheeler, a seventy-six-year-old from Sun City, Arizona.

Why would they drive all the way to Mexico? Why spend their day in a dim waiting room, watching shadowy soap operas in a foreign language? Why tolerate the groaning of a window air conditioner churning out lukewarm gusts in the desert heat?

Why? Because they were searching. For hope.

And we search for it too.

Every day we hunt for hope, in ways we don't realize. We buy new things we *hope* will bring us joy or fulfillment. We search for love and friendship, *hoping* a new relationship will bring what the last ones didn't. Why do we vote? Work? Save our pennies? Spend our pennies? Because we're wired to hope.

And none of these hopes deliver, at least not entirely.

- The weight loss shake doesn't slim our waistline.
- "The secret to working from home and making $20,000 a month" . . . never pays off its shipping fee.
- The retirement earned after forty years is so . . . empty.
- The job that seemed so exciting gets so . . . old.

Other times, we grasp for weightier hopes: The hope of self-help. The hope of religion. The hope of "enough faith, and my problems will all go away." And for so many of us, the hope of distraction. We numb our aching souls with constant busyness.

Our hopes grow from our inadequacies. No matter how strong we are, we all have some situations we are powerless to control: health problems, relationship tensions, addictions, emotional unrest, financial burdens—the list goes on. For each of these, we *hope*.

Like fish in an aquarium with plastic plants, we swim in a world of plastic hopes.

Some days we realize how desperate we are for hope:

- when we're lying in the hospital
- when we're returning, alone, to the cemetery
- when a loved one storms out of the house, or we lose our income

Other days, in the busyness of life, we ignore our appetite for hope. But when we slow down, we sense an underlying emptiness. There it is—our hunger for hope.

God designed you for more than an endless, frustrating search. He designed you to *find* hope. And He stepped into our world to deliver it. It's what Jesus was talking about when He said, "Come to me, all you who are weary and burdened, and I will give you rest."[1]

He invites the weary and the burdened to come to Him. And what does He promise? ". . . *you will find rest for your souls.*"[2]

What a claim. What a hope! Rest for our souls. Relief from the tension we carry in our necks, shoulders, and spirits. It sounds too good to be true. After all, we've heard plenty of hope-giving promises that don't deliver.

I was opening my mail when the cover of *Time* magazine caught my eye. It shouted, in giant type, "How to Cure Cancer." The cover story carried an even more dramatic subtitle: "Yes, it's now possible to cure cancer—thanks to a new cancer dream team."

*Wow,* I wondered. *Had cancer been cured while I was watching TV? Had I missed the big story?*

The good journalists of *Time* magazine wouldn't lie to us common folk, would they? The nation's leading news magazine wouldn't broadcast a false hope, just to sell a few magazines, right?

Wrong. I opened the magazine to learn that, actually, cancer had *not* been cured. Some headline editors preyed on our hunger for hope. They fed us beautiful, clever words—that were empty.

With age, we wise up. We hear words like "hope" or "strength for the weary," and we shrug. Or we cringe. *It's not a real hope,* we think. *Just another sales pitch. Another TV preacher fishing for money. More religious hot air.*

Is Jesus Christ and His message of new life just another false hope for the gullible? How about His claim to make weak people strong? Nice, clever words, sure. But might they be as empty as that *Time* magazine cover? As foolish as the magical "stem cell" injections in Mexico?

God brought this book into your life because He wants you to know that His hope is real. He does have good plans for you. He even has plans to turn your hurts and weaknesses into something good—impossible as that seems. God is reaching out to you today to give you real and meaningful hope that makes sense in the grit of your struggles and hurts.

When God came down among us in the person of Jesus, He didn't come to sell a shiny false hope. He didn't come, like so many hucksters, to *get* for Himself.

He came to *give.* Jesus spoke of an "eternal life" that begins after we leave this earth. He also spoke of "abundant life" right here and now. Abundant life, we will see, is not a life free from problems as much as it is a life full of peace and a power that outmuscles our problems.

Jesus came to give us "a living hope."[3] Think about that—a hope that breathes and grows and has muscle. A hope that can advance and fight and fend off the difficulties in your life. Isn't that so different from the withering, shrinking facades of hope we've experienced in the past?

Jesus came to give you a life that even death cannot take away. An entirely new sort of life that begins with peace here in this broken world and then continues in a better place where there are no hucksters, no false hopes, no deaths, no pains, and no tears.

Maybe you opened this book because you've already experienced God's power in your life, and you want more of it. If so, you've come to the right place. On our journey, we will venture deep into the life-giving hopes of heaven.

Or maybe you're skeptical. Maybe you doubt this claim that God's strength can blossom through your hurt and weakness. That's okay. In my own moments of pain, I often doubt these promises too. But my doubt has not stopped God from building a firm foundation under my life through the truths expressed in these pages.

Whether this is your first sip of God's strength or a return to the well for another gulp, here you will find the pure, concentrated hope of Jesus for your life today.

Together we will explore questions like:

- *If God is good, why do I have this pain or disappointment in my life?*

- *If I believe, why have I not been healed or delivered from this suffering?*

- *Does my pain mean God is mad at me? Is He punishing me?*

- *How could God possibly bring any good from this unthinkable evil?*

We will anchor our souls in the sturdy, ancient hopes that have carried people of faith for thousands of years through starvation, torture, physical pain, and emotional agony. We will learn practical ways to find God's strength in and through our weaknesses.

Whether you are a spiritual leader or not that spiritual at all, God has something for you in this promise of His strength exploding through your weakness and changing your life.

Let's journey into this mystery—that God's strength can be "perfected" in your life and in mine. Not through our highlight reels and trophy walls, but through our darkest secrets, our deepest pains, our replaying regrets, and our biggest fails.

No matter how dark your night or how deep your pit—no matter if your struggles are past, present, or building on the horizon—your heavenly Father wants to give you a front-row seat as He works good in the midst of your difficulty. He is a God who "gives strength to the weary and increases the power of the weak."[4]

# PART 1

# STRENGTH OF HOPE

*The Gifts of Prison*

# CHAPTER 1

# Living Proof of Heaven's Strength

The LORD upholds all who fall
and lifts up all who are bowed down.
*Psalm 145:14*

*When difficulties rock our world,* it's normal to think, *If life is bad, then God must be mad.* But that, we are going to see, simply is not true.

The truth is that God still loves you, even when your life is bad—*especially* when your life is bad. Like a loving parent, God hurts with you. When He sees you suffering or struggling, He generously offers His compassion to you. Scripture promises, "The LORD is close to the brokenhearted and saves those who are crushed in spirit."[1]

In the last seventeen years, Joy Veron has learned to find God's strength in unthinkable tragedy. I first learned about Joy when I Google searched "Mother's Day video." I hoped to find a video about a mom who loved her kids as they endured hardship. Instead, I found the story of a mom who continued loving her kids and loving life as she herself endures unthinkable pain.

It was a homemade video, filmed in the cozy kitchen of a lived-in home. In it, two teenage girls hold up handwritten signs, explaining an unbelievable story about their mom's love.

By the end of the video, my eyes were stinging with tears. Chloe's and Annie's handwritten signs read as follows in their Mother's Day video:

"We want to tell you a story about our mom"

"Our mom and dad got married in 1991"

"In 1992, I was born"

"A few years later, in 1994, I was born"

"And finally, in 1996, our little brother was born"

"We lived in a happy home with lots of love and laughter"

"And a mom who loved us more than the world"

"But there was an accident in 1999 that changed *everything*"

"We were on vacation with my grandparents"

"And we were going to rent a log cabin"

"It was beautiful and overlooked a huge cliff"

"We were so excited!"

"At the time, I was 7"

"I was 5"

"And our brother was 3"

"When we pulled into the driveway of the house"

"My parents and grandparents got out of the car to sign paperwork in the doorway"

"My sister, brother, and I stayed in the car and watched from the window"

"Even though my mom had her keys with her, the car somehow knocked out of gear"

"And started rolling . . ."

"Toward the cliff"

"As soon as my mom saw what was happening"

"She did the unthinkable"

"She ran in front of the SUV, determined to stop it"

"We remember the look on her face right before she went under"

"And we remember feeling the bump as we ran over her body"

"That bump saved our lives"

"It slowed the car down just enough for my grandpa to run up beside it"

"And pull the emergency brake"

"Right before we went [would have gone] over the cliff"

"The weight of the SUV on my mother's body should've killed her"

"But by some miracle of miracles"

"It didn't"

"But it did break her back"

"She is paralyzed from the waist down"

"And she will never walk again"

"But she says she wouldn't change it for the world because her 3 kids are alive and with her"

"She hasn't let her wheelchair stop her from *anything*"

"She has been at every piano recital"

"Every tennis tournament"

"And is the voice at the end of the phone when I'm away at college"

"She is our rock"

"And our best friend"

"She is the most amazing mother in the world"

"She taught us from a young age that when people stare at us because of her wheelchair"

"We should hold our head up high"

"And just stare back"

"That is what she has done with life"

"Life gave her a tough hand of cards"

"But she arranged them into something beautiful"

"Yes, she saved our lives in the accident in 1999"

"But she saves them over and over again, each and every day"

"Happy Mother's Day, Mom" (You can watch this video at IamStrongBook.com.)

Joy Veron laid down her life to save the lives of her children. She has lived the last seventeen years in a wheelchair. From getting out of bed to bathing and simple daily duties, the monotony and help-lessness of life in a wheelchair leads many into despair, bitterness, and depression. But that hasn't been the case for Joy Veron.

Everyone who knows Joy knows that hers is not a life of bitter-ness or cynicism. Instead, from her wheelchair, Joy Veron exudes a contagious love for life and for others. She exudes, as her name suggests, joy.

How is this possible? *How can she have a better outlook—from a wheelchair—than many of us have from our armchairs? How can she have such strength in such weakness?*

The answer is that Joy Veron has learned the secret we seek to learn in this book. The secret that God's strength best invades our lives through our weakness and pain. Joy Veron is living, breathing proof that God can bring good from the struggles and tragedies in our lives, if we will invite Him into our weakness and pain.

And that, Joy says, is the secret—inviting God *into* the pain. In early 2013, I wrote Joy to ask if I could use her Mother's Day video in a presentation.

Her reply captures the life skill we are pursuing for our own sufferings:

> Hi, John!
>
> I would be honored for you to use the video.
>
> About a year after my accident, I was still in rehab searching and waiting on something to make me "whole" again. I was in my bedroom early one morning listening to my young children get ready for school. I realized what a sad house we had. There was just a feeling of grief always in the air. It hit me so strongly.
>
> I realized God was there and could bring good from this

terrible event in our life, but I had to allow it and welcome the good.

While the kids were at school, I went out and bought them journals. I told them we would keep a list of the good and bad things from the accident. It wasn't long before we saw the "good" list far outweighed the "bad." In fact, it became more of a mental thing, and we eventually just made notes of it in our life. I saw my attitude change, and joy and laughter began to fill our house again.

It isn't to say that there aren't still days when we get aggravated, but I can truly say the blessings have far outweighed the negative. It wasn't until I welcomed God to bless us through something that was so difficult for our family that we began to heal.

Few of us have tasted God's strength in our sufferings the way Joy Veron has. That's not because we are short on sufferings or weaknesses. We're missing God's strength because we haven't yet "welcomed God to bless us through" our difficulty as Joy has.

God invites us to parade our wounds and weaknesses before Him, welcoming Him to touch our inadequacies and work miracles through them. When we do, we will begin seeing His power as never before.

He gives strength to the weary
and increases the power of the weak.
*Isaiah 40:29*

Joy Veron joins a prominent list of souls who acknowledged God in their suffering and, as a result, unlocked a passageway through which supernatural power entered their lives. Abraham Lincoln, Martin Luther King Jr., and Flannery O'Connor all describe finding God's supernatural strength in their lives through the passageway of personal weakness.

Paul the apostle wrote much of the New Testament. He so discovered God's supernatural strength through his suffering that he wrote, "When I am weak, then I am strong."[2] To learn more about those famous sufferers and their words about God's strength through their difficulty, see appendix 1 ("The Strongest Sufferers").

Joy Veron joined the ranks of these powerful sufferers by bringing her unthinkable pain to the loving God who "gives strength to the weary and increases the power of the weak."[3]

We can join their ranks too.

We all have weaknesses, hurts, fears, and sufferings. The old relationship wounds we try not to think about, the regrets or disappointments that knocked us down in life. The sickness or exhaustion we cannot understand.

We all walk or wheel through life with our own unique limps—a painful upbringing, trauma, or abuse; a challenging spouse; an unexpected death; a too-big nose. Miscarriage, destructive habits, broken relationships, financial strain. We shoulder these wounds every day as we move from shower to work to grocery store and back home. We are a world of limping people, each of us doing our best to hide our weaknesses, to cover them as we shuffle along.

Joy Veron offers living proof that this promise—God's strength in our weakness and suffering—is not a false hope. It is living, active, available power for your life today.

In the next chapter, I will explain how I have begun to experience God's strength in my own physical weakness. I am learning that:

God's Strength + My Weakness
Is Better Than
My Strength + No Weakness

Or for the math nuts:

God's Strength + My Weakness > My Strength + No Weakness

My natural tendency is to think I will be stronger if I can just be rid of my pain, struggle, or weakness. But I'm learning that my suffering, *when combined with God's strength*, is actually far more powerful than my own way of living in times free from suffering.

There is a quality and quantity of heaven's strength that fits into our lives only through the delivery door of our pain and weakness. Here, in Joy's words, are the moments that transformed her tragedy into victory.

- "I realized God was there and could bring good from this terrible event in our life, *but I had to allow it and welcome the good*."
- "I can truly say the blessings have far outweighed the negative. *It wasn't until I welcomed God to bless us through something that was so difficult for our family that we began to heal*."

Such a thought may seem impossible—pure fiction—to you today. But God has good plans to heal your deepest wounds and to show His goodness in your most paralyzing weakness. Hang in there with me in these pages. Together, let's watch in wonder as God works good where we never thought He could.

For every inadequacy and weakness in our lives today, God has a correlating strength and sufficiency. For every pain and evil, past or present, you can claim this promise: "You intended to harm me, but God intended it for good."[4] Join me, and let's learn how.

# CHAPTER 2

# Thorns in Our Flesh

> What, after all, is more universal to human
> experience than suffering? And what is more
> important than the perspective we bring to it?
> *Randy Alcorn*

*At the ripe old age* of twenty-seven, I experienced the signs and symptoms of a stroke, one in a string of soul-shaking, frightening episodes.

I was about to walk onto the stage to preach on a Sunday morning. Not that I was much of a preacher. I was just a young journalist who had seen Jesus' power to change lives, including my own.

A small, declining church in Prescott, Arizona, was about to close its doors. The congregation of forty invested its final savings to hire me as their "senior pastor."

I showed up with no plan except to preach God's Good News and love His people. And then God started bringing people. After the first year, we had about 120 folks. It might as well have been 120 million to us. They seemed like a huge crowd, filling our little sanctuary.

I was about to speak to these folks on a December morning in 2009, when I gathered beforehand to pray with a few close friends. As we prayed, I felt numbness creeping its way from the fingertips on my right hand up toward my face and tongue.

Small, spinning pixels of rainbow color appeared like spots in my vision, floating around like dandelion fuzzies.

"Pray for me," I told the friends.

And pray we did.

Fearful thoughts about my health pulled at my mind. I opened the deepest parts of me before God. There, I grabbed on to all the faith that I had built up in the last ten years of watching God work miracles.

> "Oh, Lord, I know you can move mountains and raise the dead. Please grant your servant strength to speak Your heart to Your people."

I prayed.

I believed.

I spoke the prayer of faith.

Then, in faith, I stepped onto the stage. I began delivering my sermon introduction with confidence. I knew God wouldn't forsake me.

I stayed closer to my notes than usual, trying to filter out the signals of numbness from my face and arm. Trying to look past the spinning bits of light to see the faces of people.

Their faces, I noticed after a bit, looked confused.

*Had I said something wrong?*

Only then did I realize, *I'm slurring my speech.* My words blurred and bled into each other as a drunken man's might, only with less coherence. These were not English words, slurred by a lazy tongue. They were the words of a broken mind.

A man from our church stepped to the stage, and strong hands escorted me away.

Some friends rushed me to the emergency room, where I writhed in agony. What began with sporadic numbness on my right side blossomed and grew into an angry, irritated tingling of pain, burning the right half of me. As it grew, so too did the vice-tightening pain in my head.

At its worst, I could not remember my name. I could not form a single word with my tongue. More frightening, I could not *think* a single word.

Unable to articulate any actual words, my inner person suffocated under this fear:

*What if I get trapped like this, unable to speak, in this pain?*

*What if I get stuck in here?*

The next day, I emerged. Hazy. Slow. But able to speak again. I did not get stuck in there. And thankfully, I have not yet. But this is my weakness. Unpredictable stroke-like episodes that arrive without notice and incapacitate me in pain when they do.

These episodes are my "thorn in the flesh," to borrow a term from the apostle Paul. I get to deal with them a few times per year. In fact, I had one of my worst ones yet when I began writing this book. It left my mind hazy, cloudy, and confused for about three weeks afterward.

A neurologist diagnosed my episodes as hemiplegic migraines— a rare, paralyzing subset of brain spasm that, he explained, afflicts only a fraction of a percent of migraine sufferers. Hemiplegics are considered the most debilitating and dangerous of migraines. Mine may be the work of blood vessel damage, resulting from Kawasaki disease, a condition I had as a toddler.

"Could it ever progress into a complete stroke?" I asked my neurologist.

"A small percentage of them do," he said.

*That's not encouraging,* I thought. *So far I'm having bad luck with these conditions that only afflict a small percentage.*

He continued. "The best thing we can do is try to prevent them and try to find the medications that minimize them for you."

Not the reassurance I had hoped for. I wanted the doctor to silence my fear of getting stuck in that place where I cannot speak, where I sense only void and pain. I hoped he would tell me it's irrational and foolish to worry.

Instead, the doctor told me I very well *could* get stuck there.

———

You likely have your own "thorn." Yours may be cancer. It may be wounds from abuse. An amputated limb. Or the amputation of the soul that is the death of a loved one.

Our thorns are not limited to physical sickness. Yours may be a recent failure or loss. Maybe your thorn is depression, exhaustion, or anxiety. The ligament-popping of a separating relationship, the emptiness of unemployment. On and on goes the list of thorns that we and our fellow humans carry around in the flesh of our souls.

The apostle Paul's thorn plagued him with constant suffering. He called it "torment."[1] Paul is a hero of the Bible; in fact, he wrote a lot of it. God greatly loved Paul, and yet the apostle lived a life of chronic physical pain. Paul knew the pain was temporary. He knew heaven awaited him, but that knowledge didn't silence his body's screaming pain sensors.

Paul eventually thanked God for his thorn in the flesh and even bragged about it: "I will boast all the more gladly about my weaknesses, so that Christ's power may rest on me . . . *For when I am weak, then I am strong.*"[2]

But I believe Paul struggled and stumbled on his way to this place of extraordinary faith. I know I still have plenty of moments when I'm not thanking God for my own thorn.

Some smiling Christians quote the words "God's power is made perfect in weakness" as if we instantly arrive at God's power without any struggle. That has not been my experience. The agony of my "thorn in the flesh" has driven me to ask many questions:

- *Is this claim of God's power through weakness just a cute Hallmark saying?*

- *Is it a cliché for Christians to recite?*

- *Is there actually a way to find God's power in my weakness, in real life?*

The Greek word Paul used for "thorn," was often translated "stake" or "stick" in ancient literature—meaning that Paul did not skip through life with an inconvenient splinter in his foot. Paul endured daily agony, a nail driven through the tender collarbone flesh of his well-being and livelihood.

Paul described himself as a man impaled with tormenting pain. Can you relate? We will all have with us, if not today then at some point in our lives, the uninvited, constant companion of pain. When I endure the worst eight to twenty hours of pain in my episodes, I swallow my prescription pills, washing them down a half-numb esophagus and spilling water from that half of my mouth.

I stick headphone earbuds in and turn on the most soothing music I know. Then I lie down. As the ability to form words escapes the grasping fingers of my mind, I try my hardest to cling to God in my inner person, in that central place that exists apart from words. I try my hardest to trust that He is good and has good plans for me.

But it is not easy.

It is normal to wonder in "thorn in my flesh" moments of agony, *If God is good and has good plans, then why do I have to endure this?*

The apostle Paul asked questions like this too. He asked, "Why is this happening?" and "Where is this pain coming from?" We know Paul asked those questions because he answers them in the letter he wrote to his friends, 2 Corinthians.

The pain of the thorn, Paul tells us, was sent by Satan.[3] Satan is *why* Paul's pain was happening, and Satan is *where* his pain originated. (This was also the case for Job, another famous sufferer of physical and emotional pain.)

Paul then asked God another question. He pleaded with God to intervene and remove the pain. Not once, but three times Paul begged God to remove his thorn of pain.[4]

Paul neither expected nor wanted God's answer. And yet, Paul accepted it. He stubbornly built his sanity around the belief that God would repurpose his temporary pain for eternal good. That's when heaven's delivery door of strength opened in Paul's life.

Paul chose to trust God's plan (heaven's strength through temporary pain) more than his own desire (immediate healing).

Trust opened the way for Paul's thorn to become an inlet of supernatural strength into his life. This is a small picture of what God is doing with all of human history—repurposing the terror of Satan's evil for the good of God's people and the glory of heaven. The repurposing happens through men and women like you and me when we choose to believe God more than we believe our pain.

———

Paul called his chronic physical pain "a messenger of Satan . . . to torment me."

Torment = ongoing, continual thrashing of pain. The constant movement of a literal thorn in our flesh brings blood to the surface. In the same way, the movement of our "thorns" as we jostle through life stirs fresh pains and questions with each setting sun.

The questions that soak the flesh around your thorn may sound like these—all questions I have heard cried, shouted, or whispered from people I love:

- *How could my child die before me? It's not supposed to work like this.*
- *Why I am hurting more than ever—after trying to do the right thing?*

- *I know I can't bring my loved one back, but why does it have to hurt so much?*
- *Why does a careless teen get pregnant at a party, and I can't?*
- *Why can't I find one doctor who will take the time to help me?*
- *Why do people who don't care about God have it so much better than I do?*

The questions that soak the flesh around my personal thorn include that moment when I mustered all my faith for healing and was left a slurring fool. I look at the expanding drops of blood around that thorn, and I can't help but wonder, *Why did God abandon me on that December morning? Wasn't I just trying to serve Him? It's not like I was plotting a murder when the encyclopedia of my brain turned into SpaghettiOs. I was preaching Scripture in church, for heaven's sake!*

And every time I endure the worst hours of pain at the peak of my episodes, I wonder, *Will this one send me into a stroke? If it does, how will my children get along without a dad? My wife, without her husband?*

Words are among the great joys of my life. Crafting words not only brings me pleasure; it also provides my family's income. And so, the idea of losing my speech, the threat of losing my ability to *think* words, let alone share them, sends tremors through my inner person.

A custom-tailored hell.

In a similar way, your thorn digs through your tender surface flesh and down into your inner person, raising your own bloodied questions. Your own custom-tailored hell.

God brought this book into your life to assure you that *He does indeed love you*, despite what you may feel or suspect in your quiet moments. In your pain, God is not torturing you.[5] He does not want to see you suffer, and He will, as you invite Him, become the Source of lasting healing for your hurts.

You need not fear any of the feelings, worries, or questions that accompany your thorn. I am daily discovering that God's presence and His answers are more comforting than the clichés we hear recited by those who mean well but do not understand our pain. Ask God to strengthen any crumb of faith you have; you will see Him galvanize your inner person as you discover His strength in your weakness.

In my exploration of Paul's thorn, I have found comforting and reassuring answers. What I did not expect to find is the veiled reality that, more than answers *about* my thorn, God wants to give me heaven's power and strength *through* my thorn.

I have learned, through my thorn, to experience the power of God in deep parts of me that I did not know existed. I am now able, because of the discoveries in this book, to access an unearthly peace during the most grueling suffering of my hemiplegic episodes. And still, I'm a beginner. There is so much more of heaven's strength waiting to enter my life through the delivery door of my weaknesses.

Heaven's power is eager to enter your life too.

I have spent plenty of hours in hospital beds. I've also spent plenty of hours sitting *next to* hospital beds—as a pastor, as a dad, and as a husband. From hospitals and funeral homes to coffee shops and airplanes, I consistently hear one repeated question from Christians: *If trusting in Jesus is supposed to make my life better, then why am I in so much pain? Isn't my life supposed to be less painful after I trust Jesus?*

I hear so many hurting people ask this question, from sincere and broken hearts. And it's no wonder. A bloating crowd of "spiritual" communicators today promise us that if only we trust Jesus, He will make our lives problem-free, *right now.* I call this message "The Myth of Problem-Free Christianity."

The problem with "problem-free Christianity" is that it is not Christianity at all. It was not the faith of Paul the apostle. He wrote most of the Christian Scriptures while living with the daily physical torment of his "thorn in the flesh."

Problem-free Christianity was also not the Christianity of Christ, who was pretty central to Christ-ianity. He endured a life of rejection, loneliness, betrayal, physical pain, social abuse, and literal torture. In my own experience with a painful health condition, and in my experience as a pastor who guides others over the slippery rocks of grief, I have discovered that Christ's solutions are sturdier and longer lasting than the sugar-empty promise of anesthetized, pain-free living in the immediate.

And Jesus relates to our pain. After all, His life on earth did not culminate on a beach, sipping a mimosa. It ended with shrieks of agony, simultaneously bleeding and suffocating to death while impaled upon a Roman torture device. *He knows how it feels to hurt, because He carried our hurts in Himself.*

Paul was one of God's most beloved and chosen people. And yet Paul agonized under severe pain in this world. Paul's thorn encourages us that pain and difficulty do not mean God is unhappy or displeased with us.

Jesus also suffered unthinkable pain, and God the Father declared of Him, "This is my Son, whom I love; with him I am well pleased."[6] (God gives many more assurances, too, that your problems do not mean God is mad at you. We will uncover those in future chapters.)

Billy Graham, one of the great communicators of God's heart, put it this way: "No matter how many sins you've committed, or whatever you've done, whatever you are—God loves you."[7]

This book aims to dismantle and disarm the destructive lie of "problem-free Christianity" for you. No more need to doubt God's love for you when life is difficult. No more fearing He disapproves when you most need His approving comfort.

Time to start finding His strength when and where you need it most. In this journey, we're piecing together the rubble in your life, mortared and held together by God's unending love.

His ability to work good from evil.

His proven promises.

His supernatural ability to bring life from death, healing from pain.

You have a greater hope than just surviving a numbed life. You have living to do. You have someone to share this adventure with. You have a purpose and a destination to keep advancing toward. You have hope. Daily strength and lifelong strength.

# CHAPTER 3

# Prisons of Pain, Chambers of Strength

> That is why I turn back to the years of my imprisonment and say, sometimes to the astonishment of those about me: "Bless you, prison!" . . . and I say without hesitation, "Bless you, prison, for having been in my life!"
>
> Soviet labor camp survivor Aleksandr Solzhenitsyn, The Gulag Archipelago

*Let's use our imaginations.* Visualize yourself alone in a medieval prison cell. A rock floor chills your feet. Walls of stone rise to a high wooden ceiling above. A heavy door, almost half a foot thick, provides the only way in or out.

This is the prison of your thorn. It's a fitting image because, whether or not we verbalize it, our weaknesses, hurts, and pains make us feel trapped. They limit our ability to function in life—sometimes physically, sometimes emotionally, mentally, or financially. At least I know my thorn can feel like a prison.

Picture yourself within those four stone walls. Imagine yourself a prisoner in that cell, serving a lengthy sentence.

One night, the heavy door to your cell opens, squeaking on its rusted hinges. In walks a surprise visitor. He begins speaking in a hushed and hurried voice, assuring you of two things.

First, he assures you that an escape plan is being formulated.

Your days in this prison are numbered. There will be a breakout for you. On hearing this, a wave of warmth moves across you.

Next, he tells you both good and bad news about your escape from the prison. The bad news is that the breakout may be years in the making. You will certainly be set free, but you will have to endure in the prison until the escape.

The good news: He will smuggle in gifts to sustain you until your escape. Not only is your future escape certain, but your daily survival is also certain.

In a hurried whisper, he explains some sustaining gifts that will be brought in for you:

**The Bread** is a daily supply of nutritious food to strengthen you. A warm loaf of bread will get sneaked in each day to *give you practical daily strength* during your time in prison.

**The Friend** is a companion who will visit you in your prison. He will comfort and *encourage you with his presence*. You can play cards, reminisce about the past, even dream about the future. The friend will come alongside you to bring strength and encouragement right into your prison. You'll feel your load lighten as you share your struggle with a strong shoulder and an understanding heart.

**The Book** explains the laws and history that built your prison. It contains a map that navigates from your prison to a better land, to which you will escape. The book *answers questions* about why you're here, how you can survive, and how you will escape.

**The Window** offers a view outside, beyond your prison walls, to green fields fertile with rich crops. Through the window, you can see the future freedom that will be yours. You can view the long, winding thread of a road that connects your present reality to your bright future. The window *gives you hope and assurance* of what lies ahead.

**The Pen and Paper** allow you to remain productive. To write letters. To compose and produce things you would likely never actually sit down and write if you were outside of prison. The pen and paper *give you purpose and meaning in your prison of pain.*

As we learn to find heaven's strength in our prisons of pain and weakness, we are going to see that God offers all of these gifts to us today. And He is in the process of breaking us out of our prisons entirely.

The subsequent parts of this book correlate to the sustaining gifts listed above:

- The bread is found in part 2: "Feeding on Heaven's Strength."
- The friend of comfort is found in chapter 6: "When You Hurt."
- The book of answers is found in part 3: "Earth's Jagged Edges."
- The window of hope is found in part 4: "Hopeful Songs in a Glorious Ruin."
- The friend of comfort returns in part 5: "Carried," which also unpacks the pen and paper in chapter 16: "Pain and Purpose."

You don't have to remember all of this now. We will open and unpack each gift in the following pages. As you open these gifts, I pray that they will give you the same supernatural strength they have given me. I can report from my own daily living that, like Paul, I have been able to enjoy these gifts in my pain and weakness.

I have come to find that any one of these gifts—available only in the prison of weakness or pain—contains a power for living that's unavailable in the grassy green fields of pain-free living. Because:

God's Power + My Weakness > My Power + No Weakness

This is what the apostle Paul had in mind when he wrote, "I am overwhelmed with joy despite all our troubles."[1] Paul experienced a joy not choked or suffocated by his surroundings or circumstances.

Paul wrote multiple books that changed human history from a literal prison, much like the one we imagined. If your prison causes you to doubt that God loves you or delights in you, remind yourself that God's favorite people often end up in prison in this life. That might sound contradictory, but it's true.

The Bible begins in Genesis with one of God's favored people, Joseph, in a prison. It ends with another, John the apostle, in an island prison. I have compiled a list of spiritual heroes who spent years in prisons of suffering. You can find it in appendix 2 ("Favored Sufferers"). If you are spiritual and suffering, it may be a great encouragement to you.

Paul found daily strength by opening his weakness to God (part 2). Paul understood God's answers to his questions about his pain (part 3). Paul drew power from a life-giving hope (part 4). Paul carried an onboard source of supernatural strength (part 5).

Through his pain, Paul formed a purpose and legacy unlike anything he could have accomplished without his thorn. Every day, millions of people around the world find strength in Paul's words, written some 1,900 years ago. Those words would not exist if Paul had not had a thorn or a prison.

A single one of these gifts can bring new joy into *your* suffering and struggle. Together, they transform your prison into a private chamber of answers, hope, strength, comfort, and purpose.

# PART 2

# FEEDING ON HEAVEN'S STRENGTH

*The Bread and the Friend of Comfort*

# CHAPTER 4

# *Children in the Universe*

———

Little ones to Him belong—
They are weak, but He is strong.
*Anna Bartlett Warner, "Jesus Loves Me"*

*My son Jack is four years old* and growing fast. Each new day, Jack emerges stronger, smarter, more sensitive, and, at times, more stubborn. I cannot put into words the affection, admiration, and love I have for this stouthearted, blue-eyed boy. My son, Jack.

I'm not a perfect father, but I do my best to communicate these feelings to Jack. I communicate my interest in him by spending time with him, by listening to him, and sometimes by just telling him how proud I am of him.

Jack fell asleep in my arms or next to me, every night, for the first two years of his life. Usually he fell asleep after a nighttime ritual that went like this:

- a bedtime story (adventures involving steam locomotive trains or old cars)
- a bedtime prayer (I used to pray them; now he does)
- the singing of some favorite songs

Jack knows I love him. But at four years old, he has no idea just *how much* I love him.

Neither do I. Increasingly I find that, when under stress at work or when feeling stuck in a writing project, the most gratifying thing for me in all the world is to simply be with Jack and his younger sister, Zoey (with whom I now get to sing those bedtime songs).

Last night, I took Jack to see a new Disney-Pixar movie. We walked in and discovered we had the entire theater to ourselves.

Jack asked, "Daddy, since it's just us in here, can I run around?"

"Absolutely," I said. "The place is ours."

Jack ran up and down the stairs, his blond flop of hair flapping as he jolted up and down, right and left. He zipped through the empty aisles, testing about forty of the ninety seats before returning to sit next to me in the back row, his original choice of seats.

I half watched the previews for upcoming family films and half watched Jack bolting through the rows. Him running with such carefree abandon, such freedom. Such pure childhood.

There's a strength unlike any other strength in the boldfaced, carefree confidence of an innocent child thriving under the safety of caring parents.

———

Sometimes I tell new friends, "Jack has two speeds: run and sleep."

So everything seemed normal on a recent Sunday afternoon when Jack went zipping around the backyard, pushing toy cars, climbing trees, and jumping off the playhouse. Jack had been running a slight fever the night before. But he'd been acting normal all day, so we hadn't thought to check his temperature. My wife decided to call him inside and take his temperature, just to be safe.

The first thermometer we used indicated Jack had a temperature of one hundred and (wait for it) *seven*. 107 degrees Fahrenheit! We swiped that thermometer across his forehead two more times, figuring it was a fluke. Twice more the digital screen read 107.

"That thermometer must be broken," I said. "Let's get the old under-the-tongue one."

One minute later, the under-the-tongue thermometer beeped. It read, 106.5. Three times in a row it read 106.5.

"Jack, are you hurting anywhere, buddy?"

"Nope. Can I go back outside and play?"

"Sorry, buddy, we gotta get you cooled down."

We stripped off Jack's shirt, positioned a fan's breeze directly on him, and placed a cloth icepack on his head. We gave him both ibuprofen and Tylenol.

Then I called a physician friend.

"With a fever that high he could have seizures," she said. "You need to get him right over to the emergency room."

So we did.

At the emergency room, the triage nurses kept marveling that they had never seen a child with that high a fever acting so happy. Jack's mom and I hadn't either. Then again, we had never seen a fever that high, period.

After more drugs and cooling, Jack's fever dropped to 104.5. Since Jack reported no pain or symptoms, the doctors wanted to run some tests.

And Jack was having a blast. He and I were not sitting on a hospital bed, he told me, but on a steam locomotive. And it was my job to dig the coal. Jack was a great sport when he stood alone in a cold room for his chest X-ray. He only smiled and laughed when another doctor poked a tiny stick into his ear canals. She called it "the world's smallest spoon." Jack just loved that.

He might as well have been in Disneyland. He was having so much fun. Then a less experienced nurse came into Jack's room. In a fraction of an instant, her words changed the mood.

"You're not gonna like this," she told Jack. "I have to do something to you that you're not gonna like."

I looked at my wife. We were both thinking the same thing:

*Oh no, you don't get cooperation from this strong-willed child by telling him he's "not gonna like" what you're about to do to him.*

The medical terror she predicted should actually have been the easiest of all Jack's tests, a simple Q-tip of saliva from Jack's throat. Given the right imaginary scenario (race car driver health screening, perhaps), Jack would have happily complied.

But the mood turned the moment the nurse told Jack he wouldn't like it.

We were no longer dealing with a compliant, fun-loving explorer.

Now we were dealing with a warrior.

Jack now believed this mob of adults intended to inflict pain on him. Indeed, by our own words, we adults had claimed a plot of cruel and unusual suffering that he was "not gonna like."

It took four of us to hold him down. The scene must have looked like something from a low-budget horror movie. Jack writhing, struggling, kicking, and flailing every limb—his every neck and back muscle resisting as we pressed against his will.

And then, in came the woman who told Jack he would "not like" what she was gonna do to him. Jack—his arms and legs restrained—began spitting all over her.

She got her saliva sample, all right. All over her face and shirt she got it.

Now, while I don't condone Jack's spitting on the nurse, I also don't blame the little guy. What would you do if someone twice your size said, "You're not gonna like what I'm about to do to you"? And then, a whole gang of towering giants, including your most trusted protectors, turned on you, restraining you like a wild animal?

It didn't matter how many times I told Jack, "This isn't gonna hurt. It's just to help you." He had been told otherwise. His view of us had shifted. His four-year-old mind could not understand how such terror could possibly be in his best interest.

If we love our children, at times love requires us to hold them down while they get stabbed with a needle or while they watch their own blood escape into a vial. These moments are for me the most heartbreaking moments of parenthood. When loving your child requires you to do something they interpret only as pain and punishment.

In those emergency room moments, our children feel entirely betrayed by us. Their providing protectors suddenly team up with strangers in a scheme to inflict unimagined harm.

We, knowing more than a four-year-old, understand that this medical test or that treatment provides the care they need. We know the temporary suffering will lead to lifelong health. But they cannot see what we see. They have no idea we are guiding them into torture, not because we want to see them suffer, but because we love them and want their best.

Jack felt betrayed and punished by me, even though I was trying to help him. In that emergency room, I realized how often we children of God, in our pain, feel the same way toward our heavenly Father. Betrayed. Punished. Abandoned.

In our suffering and difficulty, we, like Jack, find it difficult to believe that our Father is good, caring, and on our side.

We hear about God the Father's goodness and love toward us, but we struggle to actually believe it. We especially struggle to think of Him as good when we find ourselves pinned down by troubles. When strangers attack us. In that fraction of an instant when our fun-and-games life turns into a horror scene of medical testing and torture.

Despite facts we learn *about* God, most of us doubt whether God the Father can really be trusted when nobody is looking. Maybe He can be trusted with *other* people's lives, sure, but not with *my* pain, not with *my* retirement, not with *my* children. I'd better keep an eye on things for myself.

Alone at a traffic light or drifting off to sleep, we wonder if God has abandoned us. Given up on us. Left the building.

God wants you to know this in your pain: First, you *are* loved by your heavenly Father, despite what you may feel. And also, even when it feels as though God has abandoned you or is torturing you, He is actually still *with* you, *for* you, and feeling for you—more than you could ever understand.

When I think of the compassion and heartbrokenness I felt for my son, Jack, as those nurses, doctors, and I myself held him down against his will, I cannot put into words the sympathy I had for him. And in the same way, your heavenly Father tells you He is "close" to you when you are "brokenhearted" (Psalm 34:18). He has compassion on you. He hurts with you when you hurt. He holds you as you hurt. He loves you, despite the pain, betrayal, or doubt you feel.

It takes great faith for us to believe we are the four-year-olds and that our Father is not intentionally harming us. It takes great faith for us to trust that, far out beyond what we can see or imagine, He is actually in the process of repurposing these temporary pains for our eternal good.

In a very real sense, Jack cannot fully understand the comparison of lifelong health and a temporary shot or saliva swab. He is a bright boy, but four-year-old minds cannot comprehend time and health in the way mature adult minds can. In a similar way, faith reveals that our mature adult minds cannot comprehend time, health, pain, or redemption like the infinite mind of our good, caring, and loving Father can.

"Unless you change and become
like little children, you will never
enter the kingdom of heaven."
*Jesus, Matthew 18:3*

The tiny acorn of an oak contains all the data and ingredients needed to produce a towering tree with dozens of branches, thousands of leaves, tons of hardwood, and a galaxy of roots. All that, and yet it's small enough to fit into a squirrel's cheek.

Jesus' model prayer, known as the Lord's Prayer, is a similar pint-size container of universe-size truth. In it, we find the power for a lifetime of following Christ through a fallen world. And it's small enough for little creatures like us to carry it with us.

Acorns become mighty oaks by soaking in water, sunlight, and soil, one day at a time. We will become mighty oaks of faith when the ingredients of the Lord's Prayer soak into our souls, one day at a time, through the various drenching storms and drought-dry summers of life.

This was Jesus' method for syphoning heaven's strength through the dimensions of the universe and into His daily life on earth.

The Lord's Prayer starts with two words: "Our Father."

But here's the catch: You can know *about* Jesus' way of drawing on heaven's strength (praying in the manner of the Lord's Prayer) without ever once *experiencing* heaven's strength.

That's because, like Jack in the emergency room, most of us have a fear barrier blocking our connection to the strength available through our relationship to our heavenly Father.

The barrier is that, in our deep inner person, we do not actually believe our Father is always good toward us in the details of our lives. We do not actually feel, at gut level, that He is looking out for us in our difficulties—at least not the way *we* would, not when we feel pinned down in life. Many of us suspect, if we're honest, that we are more loving as parents toward our own kids than God the Father is toward us.

And almost all of us, if we are honest, think that if *we* sat at the controls of the universe, we could do a slightly better job of running our lives than God does.

Now, God has patience for that sort of thinking. But it's we who suffer when we don't trust God as much as we trust ourselves. If we don't push ourselves to properly redefine our Father for who He is, we will miss out on the fullness of strength available to us as His kids.

Until we deal with this core doubt, we miss out on the fearless, childlike way of life that Jesus had as He journeyed through this sin-infected planet. Remember Jack running through the movie theater so carefree, fearless, unaware of any worries in the world? God's children can live with similar confidence, even as we pick our way through the rubble of a jagged and broken world.

But we won't live that way until we learn to see our heavenly Father as the good Father He actually is.

This is an overgrown, infected wound in our souls—our distorted view of the Father, our unintentionally bending Him to the image of our human authorities. Entire books have been written on this (*Abba's Child* by Brennan Manning is a good place to start). We return to our spiritual childhood when we differentiate our true heavenly Father from our earthly authorities and their mistakes, distance, abuse, or plain old human quirks.

We will not exhibit the fearless mind-set of Jesus on earth until we learn His strength of relationship to the heavenly Father. Strength of relationship goes beyond our understanding or even our hope, because it's a strength that goes beyond ourselves. It rests on Someone greater. Someone who sees more. Someone who has a better plan. It puts us, like children, onto the shoulders of Someone so much stronger. The result is an inner rest and relaxation beyond anything we can understand, comprehend, or work up in meditation. Why? Because it does not come from within us.

At its peak, this strength of relationship would look like four-year-old Jack saying, as those emergency room doctors and nurses approach, "Okay, Dad, if you say this is for my good, I can handle it." He would still be afraid, but he would trust. That's not natural. That's not normal. Especially in time of crisis. But it's what strength of relationship *can* look like in your life and mine.

My challenge to you is this: Right now, tell God that you want to break through the barrier of fear. Tell Him you want to trust Him with your life and your hurts, even when it means trusting Him more than you trust yourself.

Next, at a heart level, ask God to help you see Him as different from past parents or authorities who hurt you, neglected you, or let you down. Tell God you want to know Him for who *He* is. That you want to have a trusting, childlike faith in His goodness and love toward you. It's as simple as saying:

> God, I want to get to know who *You* actually are as my heavenly Father. Please help me separate You from the human authorities in my life. I want my relationship with You, God, to be the unshakable strength in my life. I want to know You, not as I *assume* You are, but as You *actually* are. I want to live for You, as Jesus did. I want to daily draw strength from my relationship to You, heavenly Father, just like Jesus did.

Jesus' extraordinary life grew from His strength of relationship with the Father. Jesus referred to Himself as "Son" more than any other way. He constantly filled His inner person with heaven's strength.

The doctors never did figure out what sickness caused Jack's little body to fight so aggressively, with its 107 degree temperature. They put him on a strong antibiotic, hoping it would do the trick.

It did. After a few days, Jack's fever dropped to 99. A few more days, and the fever vanished entirely.

It broke my heart to hold Jack down against his will in that emergency room. He has now seen that all the pain resulted in his healing. But I'm pretty sure that if we repeated the scenario tomorrow, Jack would still throw a fit at the moment a nurse told him, "You're not gonna like what I'm about to do to you."

As we journey through this fallen world, we all have times when life says, "You're not gonna like what I'm about to do to you." Like that nurse, life could benefit from some lessons in bedside manner.

Our aim is to learn to live as confident, carefree children of a good Father who never forsakes us. We're learning to trust Him, even when life lacks bedside manner. Because He is there with us, seeing farther than we can see, planning things far better than we can imagine.

Your Father says this about you, *"For I know the thoughts that I think toward you, says the* LORD, *thoughts of peace and not of evil, to give you a future and a hope."*[1]

Do you believe it?

I once sat at the bedside of a dying woman who believed that verse with all her fragile, ninety-four-pound being. She believed it, even as I placed small ice cubes in her mouth because she had grown too weak to drink—her throat dry in the final breaths of death.

Earlier, she had asked me to keep reading that verse to her, Jeremiah 29:11.

*"For I know the thoughts that I think toward you, says the* LORD, *thoughts of peace and not of evil, to give you a future and a hope."*

As I continued reading those words to her, I saw peace fill her. How gently she left this world of trouble. How triumphantly she stepped—able-bodied, strong, and young again—into her true home, where things are pain-free, where her husband of sixty years was waiting with arms open in a warmer embrace than anything she had known on earth.

We are praying and working in these next chapters to gain her faith in the heavenly Father. We are maturing our trust of God. So that, even when life pins us down and starts jabbing things into our throats, we will know that our Father is good, that He has our best in mind. He is delivering us out from here. He will sustain us down here. And He is with us, hurting with us in our pain.

We are learning to live as children who are deeply loved. We are learning to live with confidence that every temporary suffering will lead to eternal good, if we just stay near "our Father."

Even when it hurts.

*Especially* when it hurts.

CHAPTER 5

# The Key and the Hammer

"Give us today our daily bread.
And forgive us our debts,
    as we also have forgiven our debtors.
And lead us not into temptation,
    but deliver us from the evil one."

*Jesus, Matthew 6:11-13*

*You had to take a boat* to get there. No roads led to the cabin.

One road led to the end of Lake Matinenda in northern Ontario, Canada. Just a few ticks north of the Great Lakes, Matinenda is a big, big body of water—some 8,813 acres, not including the waterways that connect it to additional large lakes. My great-aunt Phyllis had a little cabin hidden away on its eighty-seven miles of shoreline.

As a boy, every summer I waited and waited until we packed for Canada. After a full day of driving, it took thirty minutes in a speedboat to cross the massive lake and find our tiny cabin, huddled under the thick green of the wooded shore.

We usually got to the cabin in late spring or early summer.

If you're ever the first person to such a cabin, you'll need more than just a key to get inside. Such cabins so close to the lake can see three to five feet of snow in the winter. And when the top of the lake freezes into a massive ice rink, the local snowmobile riders like to rattle the door handles on the cabins, hoping for an easy winter shelter.

If your cabin is not well secured, it will make a nice party shack for a group of snowmobilers. And they don't often leave the place better than they found it.

As a result, each summer's closing-up procedures included the literal boarding up of the cabin. If you've seen pictures of folks boarding up houses for a hurricane, you've got the idea.

My dad would hammer large, precut pieces of wood (each measured to correspond with a door or window) onto the outside of the cabin. The covers kept out the gigantic snowdrifts, the snowmobilers, and the wildlife.

It was always a sad ritual at the end of a summer to hold those big covers in place. Or, as I got older, to nail them myself into their well-worn slots near each window and door. At last, with everything closed and locked up, we nailed the giant wooden cover over the front door.

But what a thrill in the spring or summer to undress the cabin! To grab the old, rusty hammer out of the boat and be the first to pry the layers of protection off. Yellow-warm sunlight beaming in, lighting planks and tables that hadn't seen sun in months.

I remember as a boy running immediately into the dark of the cabin and watching from inside the odd distortions of sunlight struggling in. Rays of yellow and red penetrating into the dim dark as my dad and older brothers pried the wooden coverings off windows and doors.

That picture—that *need*—to cover up our openings for protection. It's a fitting picture of the wounds, hurts, and pains in our lives.

As toddlers, before we learn to talk or walk, we begin learning to cover the places where people hurt us. We learn that hostile forces, snowmobile riders, or worse will take advantage of us if we don't cover our flaws, our worries, our insecurities.

We further learn it in elementary school—this need to cover our vulnerabilities. Then with each passing season, life wounds us in more creative ways in deeper parts of our self. We respond with more creative coverings, concealing any place where anyone could harm us. Year after year, we add more protective layers. And life becomes a perpetual boarding up of ourselves. Of our souls.

Each spring, as we peeled the protective covers off the cabin, the Canadian Maple planks inside saw light for the first time in ten months. Under the coverings of our souls, some of our wounds have not seen light for ten *years*, or more.

Beneath the religious clutter we associate with it, the Lord's Prayer is little more than prying off protective covers, the opening and parading of human weaknesses before a Father who is loving and good.

The disciples knew where Jesus got His power. It was through prayer. That's why they made this request of Him: "Lord, teach us to pray" (Luke 11:1). They weren't being religious when they asked for the prayer lesson; they were being hungry.

They wanted the same power Jesus had.

If you think of the lengthy prayers that preachers, politicians, and leaders bellow out with their eyes half closed, it's comical to note the brevity of Jesus' model prayer. No fluff or pomp. No chest beating.

The entire pinky of a prayer folds into two easy halves:

1.  Jesus aligns Himself with the Father.
2.  And then Jesus asks.

That's it. He aligns. And He asks.

Quite specifically, quite gutturally, with vulnerable unveiling, He asks.

## Align and Ask

In the words "Our Father," Jesus *aligns* with God as His identity, family, home, purpose, and security. Then Jesus' model prayer simply *asks* for daily needs.

They are *human* needs.

They are *normal* needs.

And He heaves them up to heaven as *specific* needs:

| | |
|---|---|
| our hungers | "give us today our daily bread" |
| our shames and obligations | "forgive us our debts" |
| our hurts and strained relationships | "as we also have forgiven" |
| our temptations and tendencies | "lead us not into temptation" |
| our need for protection | "deliver us from the evil one" |

You may think the Lord's Prayer has little to do with the hurts and wounds you've boarded up or covered over in your life. But in the Lord's Prayer, Jesus encourages us to pry the coverings off our most human needs.

The thorn or hurt that brought you to this book may take a lifetime to open to heaven's warm, healing rays of light. That's okay. But you can begin by opening some of your smaller hurts. By prying away some of the window coverings.

In such unveiling, the rays of heaven flit into the stale darkness of our hurts. Jesus is teaching us to daily unveil our weaknesses before our Father, who is the One we can fully trust.

And Jesus does not list churchy or religious weaknesses. He talks about the most real and gut-level feelings in our lives:

- the hunger in our stomachs
- the guilt in our hearts
- the relational conflicts that keep us awake
- the temptations that gnaw like a rat on our tattered wills to do right

More often, we talk about these basic needs on Facebook than on our knees. Other times, we ignore our basic appetites and cavities, hoping they will go away if we refuse to acknowledge them. When did you last ask God to help with one of these?

- jealousy
- fear
- embarrassment
- shame
- debt
- hurt
- temptation
- personal attack

Jesus teaches us to pray, "Lord, I'm tempted to lust after that person." "Lord, I'm tempted to gossip about that friend." "Lord, I'm tempted to covet that home, to worry about the future. Will you please help me with my very real needs?"

He's teaching us to pray, "God, today I hunger to be loved—really loved and known. Help fill that hunger, please."

Or, "God, after all these years, it *still* hurts that he did that." Or, "Lord, I cannot love my spouse the way You want me to." Or, "Father, it's another day, and once again, I don't understand why I have cancer. I need Your help."

Jesus is showing us that if we will pry away our protective coverings, the yellow-warm beams of heaven will gently warm our inner lives. But that warming light has only one way to enter: through the unveiled openings of daily weakness.

Your Father wants to hear about your actual temptations, your real hungers. He wants to hear about your medical worries, about how you miss your loved one, about your deepest fears and wounds and insecurities.

If you're tired, He wants to hear about it.

If you're put off by the way a person treated you, He wants to hear about it.

Think of the implications of the Lord's Prayer:

| | |
|---|---|
| *When you're hungry, He's listening* | "give us today our daily bread" |
| *When you're ashamed, He's listening* | "forgive us our debts" |
| *When you're hurting, He's listening* | "as we also have forgiven" |
| *When you're tempted, He's listening* | "lead us not into temptation" |
| *When you're attacked, He's listening* | "deliver us from the evil one" |

Not only is He listening, but He is also inviting. He is waiting to warm you, to light the dust-covered, dark areas of your soul.

Have you ever seen a wounded animal? For my twelfth birthday, I got a massive dog named Casey. She was a white Samoyed sled dog. Picture a Siberian Husky in all snow-white fur, and you've got the idea.

Casey was full-grown when we got her from the animal shelter. Because of some trauma in her past, she feared people. I remember a time when Casey got a small stick impaled into the flesh of her paw, between the dark, black pads.

Injured animals don't like humans touching their wounds. As much as Casey and I had bonded, she kicked and tried to limp away whenever I reached for the stick that had impaled her foot. Eventually, I had to pin her down in order to help her. Here's the point:

*When you feel pinned down by God, you can know that He actually wants to help you.*

Wounded animals instinctively suspect an approaching human will do further harm to their wound, even when we are trying to help. Many of us have the same false instincts about God. We fear God has abandoned us with our thorns. Or worse, we suspect God Himself wants to see us suffer. We worry that He is some sort of evil torturer.

Instead, Scripture tells us that God is compassionate toward the suffering, the single source of all compassion in the universe, "the God of all comfort, who comforts us in all our troubles."[1]

Looking at the guttural needs Jesus lists in the Lord's Prayer, we see it for what it is. Us lying down next to a good and loving Master. Us offering up the thorns and sticks that have stuck their ways into the tender pads of our souls. Us choosing to trust His strong and gentle hands, even as we tremble in pain and fear.

What if we actually prayed this way?

What if we actually attempted to trust our Father this way?

I think we would limp less.

We ask for massive, broad healing, then give up when it doesn't immediately come. But have we asked for strength today to follow God through the sickness of this world and to remain faithful to Him in it?

We ask to not hurt in our grief. But have we asked God to be our comforter, our friend, and our strength, to walk with us as companion in our grieving today?

In one hundred other matters, we can get more specific, more human, and more daily in the unveiling of our deepest hungers and insecurities.

"God, I need strength, if my body is gonna be this sick, to not be grumpy."

"Help me see what *You* want me to do in this situation. And I also need the strength to *do* it."

"I need *Your* love for my children and spouse today because my love is too shallow. Give me Your love for them, I ask."

When I began serving as a pastor, I thought I needed to look a certain way. I knew God didn't need me in a particular kind of clothing, but I figured the people might. In a similar way, I thought the people needed a leader who was always smiling, always happy.

(God has since taught me that I'm not the perfect leader they need. *He* is.) I remember, back in those days, many a long handshake line, many a long Sunday, many a graduation party or wedding, at which I would continue smiling and nodding and laughing.

Afterward, my wife and I would collapse into the car. Once the car doors slammed shut, I would unveil the layers of mask. "I'm so exhausted," I would tell her.

Most of us do this in one way or another. We put on the appropriate face for the appropriate folks. And most of us have experienced that moment when, with closest friends or family, we let down the fake smiles. In that moment, we talk about what's *actually* going on beneath our protective coverings. "I'm hungry." Or, "I'm exhausted." Or, "I can't believe that old codger said that. What a jerk!"

This is where God wants to be with us—in the closeness of the inner circle, after the car doors close. Invite Him in among your most trusted friends and family. That's where He wants to be. He wants to hear about your exhaustion, your fatigue, your hunger, your temptation, your 101 daily needs.

He wants you to bring Him in on every inadequacy so that you discover in Him adequacy. You can invite Him in now.

*What actual gut feelings, fatigues, and intuitions do you tell only to your closest friends?* That is where Jesus lived His prayer life. That is where the strength of heaven rushed into His human, earthly life. God wants to be that same sort of friend and companion to you.

Your Father is waiting to provide enough comfort, enough strength, enough companionship, for every one of your daily needs.

———

When my children—Jack, four, and Zoey, two—wake up in the morning, they don't run to the checkbook. They don't dress for work or hurry to the office desk to pay bills. They run to Mom and Dad. They know that in Mom and Dad all their needs will be met today.

And then in confidence they declare, "I'm hungry." Or, "I'm thirsty."

We try to teach our kids manners, yes. But we invite the candid unveiling of their daily needs. Why? Because as loving parents, we exist to meet their daily needs. We delight in meeting their needs.

In the same way, you can begin running to your Father each morning. Aligned as His child and eager for Him, you can begin asking.

Ask confidently.

Ask specifically.

Ask for your needs.

Ask for every hunger in your stomach, in your mind, in your body, and in your heart.

Ask daily.

The longer your list of daily needs, the better. (You simply have more doors and windows through which His light can shine in as you pry off the coverings.)

You have a loving and strong Father. He is eager to hear your needs and supply His strength in the grit and groans of your weakness.

Ask Him for help with your raw human desires, impulses, and fears.

Jesus' secret strength came through this sort of prayer. Prayer that was unveiling, honest, and friend-like toward a good and listening Father.

Jesus gave us the keys to the kingdom.

So come boldly.

And don't forget your hammer.

# CHAPTER 6

# When You Hurt

If we have not quiet in our minds, outward
comfort will do no more for us than a
golden slipper on a gouty foot.
*John Bunyan*

*Did you ever have* a mean science teacher? I did. He contributed to the most embarrassing day of my teenage years, when I stood crying in the hallway of my high school.

I attended a strict private school, and I was a class clown. Those two did not mix well. I huddled in the back row of most classes, drawing cars or motorcycles on my notes and cracking intermittent jokes during the lectures. I perpetually got in trouble for talking in class. And most times, I deserved it.

But I'll never forget one day in my science class. The teacher, an overcompensating macho type, had his back to the class while he drew on the chalkboard at the front of the room. With the teacher's back to us, some of the kids started laughing and giggling about who knows what.

For once, possibly the first time in my life, I was *not* the kid talking during the lecture. When the teacher heard the laughter, he whipped around, pointed at me, and shouted, "Dickerson!—detention!—see me after class!"

I looked up from the dirt bike I had been drawing on my notes. Mouth gaping wide. I hadn't been talking; I hadn't even been paying attention to anyone who was talking (teacher included, until he yelled). I had been wrongly accused by a big, intimidating authority figure.

I spent the rest of the class assuring myself that I could reason with the teacher. *Maybe show him the motorcycle. Yeah, that's a good idea.* Somehow I had to explain that, for once in my life, I was innocent.

The end-of-period bell rang, and I made my way to the front of the room. I tried to tell him, "Yeah, I know I clown around a lot, but you have to believe me. I'm not a liar. I really wasn't the one talking this time. I was minding my own business; I promise."

"Liar," he told me. "You're always making trouble. Here's your detention."

Something about the ferocity and tenacity of his reaction made the injustice all the worse. For once, I was really and fully innocent. He not only disbelieved me; my declaration made him even angrier. Somehow all those things converged with my changing teenage hormones and just broke my little fourteen-year-old spirit.

Next thing I knew, I was standing by my locker in the high school hallway, just crying.

I opened my locker door and buried my head in that little square foot of privacy, hoping nobody would see me there. I knew my tears would only invite mockery, but I couldn't hold them in.

I stood there, eyes closed. Salty, warm water pressed tight under my eyelids. My right hand gripped the edge of the locker door, a thin metal barrier between me and the world from which I desperately wanted to hide.

Then I felt a hand on my shoulder.

I looked up.

It was my older brother, Paul. He put his arm around me. "You're gonna be okay, buddy."

I was a freshman, among the new runts at high school.

He was a senior, the established ruling class.

I was crying, imploding, really.

He was strong.

He came alongside me. And he just stood there—*with* me.

Scripture describes God's Spirit in this same posture—with His arm around us—if we will seek this comfort in our lives. The Holy Spirit longs to encourage us in our difficulty.

—

The Spirit of God strengthened early believers to do mighty things for God. Then, when those same believers faced rejection, persecution, and murder for telling the world about Jesus, the same Spirit *encouraged* them.

Scripture tells us the church (tens of thousands of Christians at this point) "was strengthened . . . and encouraged by the Holy Spirit."[1]

I've met some strong people in my life. NFL athletes, Fortune 500 CEOs, power politicians.

I've met some encouraging people too. Sweet mothers, tender feelers, people whose words build your spirit and confidence.

Rarely do the two—unusual strength and sincere encouragement—combine in the same person. When they do, you sense something of the divine in it. And that's how God's Spirit is. The same Spirit who strengthens us when we are powerless also comforts us when we hurt.

In the bloodstained beginning of Christianity, Christ's followers were encouraged by the Holy Spirit. The ancient Greek term translated "encouraged" means "to come alongside" or "to cling to." The Holy Spirit is the One who comes alongside you, who clings to you and comforts you—if you will have Him.

Jesus used this name for the Spirit, when he told the disciples, "It is for your good that I am going away. Unless I go away, the Advocate [the One who comes alongside] will not come to you; but if I go, I will send him to you."[2]

Sometimes I wish Jesus were still physically here on planet Earth. I wish He could ride shotgun while I drive to work. He could give me advice. We could tell jokes. Perhaps He could immediately heal my pains. I tend to think, *I would have a stronger faith if Jesus were physically here with me.* But Jesus disagrees. Notice what He says: "It is for your good that I am going away."

*Jesus, I wonder at times how it could possibly be good for You to go away. That makes no sense. How can I be better at following You when I cannot even see You?*

Jesus answers, "Unless I go away, the Advocate will not come to you; but if I go, I will send him to you."

The Advocate Jesus speaks of is the Holy Spirit of God, the One who comes alongside Christians and clings to us in our difficulties.

Can you remember a time of tears or turmoil in your life when someone came alongside you? Put their arm around you? Hugged you? The Holy Spirit desires to come alongside you to comfort you and encourage you in the same way.

When you're hurting, confused, or doubting, the Holy Spirit eagerly waits to encourage you.

When you stumble as you try to follow Jesus, when you get discouraged, the Holy Spirit longs to help you.

## Inner versus Outer Peace

> Father of all mercy! God of all healing counsel!
> He comes alongside us when we go through
> hard times, and before you know it, he brings
> us alongside someone else who is going
> through hard times so that we can be there
> for that person just as God was there for us.
> *2 Corinthians 1:3-4 MSG*

We tend to want our peace to come from the outside into us. We want a healthy diagnosis. We want a calmed storm, a resolved conflict, a repaired problem. And that's how it will be in heaven. We'll find ourselves in a land where all that's outside of us is peace.

But until then, until we get out of this broken world (further explained in part 3, "Earth's Jagged Edges"), the things around us are guaranteed to be *un*peaceful, at least to some degree.

How ironic that we spend most our lives hunting for outer strength and outer peace. Ironic because the more you think about it and the more you watch other people, it becomes clear that you can have outer peace while lacking inner peace.

I saw this when my journalism duties took me among the extremely wealthy "one percenters" of the world. I met with people who owned multiple private jets, who owned the luxury hotels they stayed in. People for whom a collection of $400,000 cars was just another thing. And among them, I saw that every single luxury of *outer* peace does not guarantee one ounce of *inner* peace.

You can have all outer peacefulness while lacking any inner peace.

And, you can have complete inner peacefulness in the midst of complete chaos.

Given a choice between the two, well, I'll take the *inner* peace every time.

Like Paul the apostle, John Bunyan did most of his writing from jail and prison cells. He once wrote, "If we have not quiet in our minds, outward comfort will do no more for us than a golden slipper on a gouty foot."

In other words, it doesn't matter how wonderful things are externally if things are difficult internally. And, it doesn't matter how difficult things are outside if things are peaceful and strong inside.

As the Spirit comes alongside your inner person, He can give you an *internal* peace, an *internal* ease, something that money cannot buy. None of the outer luxuries of the world can produce it. The Spirit comforts us where we most need it, not in our circumstances, but in our souls.

John Ortberg put it this way:

> Easy doesn't come from the outside; easy comes from the inside. Easy does not describe the problem I will face; Easy describes the strength from beyond myself, with which I can carry my problems. If . . . you try to cultivate a life that is easy on the inside, you will be able to handle all kinds of difficult on the outside. But if you aim at having a life . . . that is easy on the outside, it will always be really hard on the inside. The more inward ease that I live in, the more outward hard I can handle.[3]

Most of us have spent our lives assuming that peace comes from the outside in, that if we could only adjust the circumstances around us, then we would have peace within. Observation tells us that our approach has been upside down. We have had it reversed. *Inward* peace is the thing to pursue.

The Holy Spirit enables followers of Christ to access such internal peace. We can be encouraged *within*, even in times of discouragement without. When everything around is falling apart, the Spirit comes alongside to give internal peace, internal strength. Internal "it's gonna be okay"—internal "*you're* gonna be okay."

Paul writes about this: "Though outwardly we are wasting away, yet inwardly we are being renewed day by day . . . since what is seen [outward] is temporary, but what is unseen [internal] is eternal."[4]

When you're troubled within, call out to the Holy Spirit. Ask Him to comfort and encourage you "in your inner being."[5] He's already listening, whether you realize it or not.

> In the same way, the Spirit helps us in our weakness. We do not know what we ought to pray for, but the Spirit himself intercedes for us through wordless groans . . . because the Spirit intercedes for God's people in accordance with the will of God.
>
> *Romans 8:26–27*

God's Spirit loves you and longs to come alongside you. He longs to comfort you and strengthen you in your inner person.

About seven years ago, my wife, Mel, whispered to me that she was pregnant with our first child.

We were both so excited. We were just kids, really, trying to make our way through a big and intimidating world. The thought of becoming parents felt overwhelming, but exciting. We hadn't figured out our marriage or future yet, but somehow we had created something amazing together. In that little person, we knew we had a future that was good and promising and full of life.

Things were going really well with the pregnancy. Until a day when I got a phone call at my office. I drove home to find Mel balled up on the couch in physical agony.

A few hours later, that pregnancy—that life—left her body.

As we sat there on the couch, it started to thunderstorm outside. In Scottsdale, Arizona, where it hardly ever rains. Sometimes reality *is* stranger than fiction. The thunderstorm knocked out the electricity in our little house.

We sat there in the dark. Just feeling like the universe was against us. I lit some candles to carry around. I made sure Mel had anything she wanted. Then I remember going into the tiny downstairs bathroom where Mel had passed the little start of a life.

In the flickering candlelight, I could see it wasn't much bigger than a goldfish. But I could discern the beginnings of a head and what would have become her eyes, or his.

I closed the door—because I didn't want Mel to hear me crying. I'll never forget the uncontrollable, heaving sobs that overtook me. Earlier, when Mel phoned to say what was happening, I didn't expect to feel anything. Now here I was, my deepest emotions uncorked by this little thing that could have been. I have never cried harder in my life.

And you know who was there with me when I was all alone in that bathroom with the door closed?

The One who comes alongside.

The calming, breathing presence of the living God.

The Spirit who comes alongside us in our troubles.

He doesn't always still our storms, but He can still *us* in the storm.

And in that thunderstorm, in that unexpected difficulty, He was there with me.

Call out to the God of comfort when you're hurting. Reach out for the One who comes alongside. When you're crying and alone. When you're hurting or confused. When you're trying to do everything right and everything is going wrong—that's when He comes alongside.

He is there for you in your hurting. The presence of the living God.

He's not yet resolving our circumstances, but He is resolving us.

He's not yet brought final peace on earth, but He can bring peace in you.

It's not heaven out there in this broken world. But He can bring pieces of heaven, foretastes, supernatural calm, to your inner being—right in the midst of your trouble.

And He'll be there for you tomorrow. He'll be with you next year.

With you at the graveside.
With you in the hospital.
With you when you're rejected.
With you when you're forgotten.
With you when you're hurting and wondering.

The Spirit brought life to creation in the beginning. He hovered over the waters. He was the breath breathed into Adam's nostrils so that man became a living thing. When our physical bodies finally break down in this evil and broken world, He will be the one to come alongside each of us who trust in Christ. To cling to us. To carry our souls to a new heaven and a new earth and a new body.

When your lungs inhale and exhale for the last time, as you breathe your last and final breath. In that moment, the Spirit who breathed life into Adam's lungs—He'll be there with you, *alongside* you as you move from this fallen world into that place where all is peace, both within *and* without.

# PART 3

# EARTH'S JAGGED EDGES

*The Book of Answers*

# CHAPTER 7

# A History of Earth's Weakness

*It's one thing to say* that God has good plans for your weakness. But our thorns raise some questions that must be answered:

- *If God really loves me, then why do I have weakness and pain at all?*
- *If God is a good Creator, then why do I have suffering in my life?*

I'd like to answer these questions by introducing you to Judy Padilla. Judy lives near Denver, Colorado. For twenty-three years, she knew her workplace wasn't perfect, but she never realized it was poisoning her.

Judy worked at Rocky Flats, a nuclear weapons production facility. The plant sprang up on a Colorado plain when the United States and the Soviet Union were stockpiling weapons during the Cold War. Rocky Flats employed about five thousand workers per shift. They milled about in eight hundred separate buildings.

Like thousands of other Rocky Flats employees, Judy knew radiation was all around her, especially when she worked the glovebox to shape the detonator of an atomic warhead. Through lead gloves, Judy could feel the heat of the plutonium-239 as she molded it.

Judy didn't realize that, due to a number of violations, her workplace was not as safe as her supervisors claimed. Invisible but deadly radiation leaked through freshly painted walls and over polished floors.

The FBI raided the facility in 1989. Investigators found that Rocky Flats violated safety guidelines and leaked radiation not only onto its 176-acre facility but also beyond into the 4,500-acre buffer zone. Officials declared Rocky Flats an environmental disaster and slated the entire plant, the size of some cities, for demolition.

Today the complex has vanished. All that remains is an empty, green, radioactive field. In the magazine *5280*, journalist Mike Kessler documents that Judy and thousands of workers like her have now contracted various forms of cancer from working at Rocky Flats. In Judy's case, after years of leaning up against the glovebox barrier to work on radioactive plutonium, she got breast cancer.

So why is there suffering and pain on planet Earth and in your life? Because spiritually, you and I live in the equivalent of Rocky Flats. We live, according to Scripture, on a planet where every molecule and mountain are contaminated by a similar, but much more deadly, radiation.

God calls this radiation sin. Planet Earth and all its inhabitants have been infected with this sickness. Death, pain, divorce, drought, famine, illness, tornadoes, hurricanes, injustice, and our own weaknesses—these are all the fallout, the result of evil that we are born into.

The Kawasaki disease that nearly killed me, at age two, the hemiplegic episodes I endure today, the fact that my body will eventually breathe a final gasp—these are all the result of spiritual contamination. Your own thorns and sufferings are also the result of a contaminating evil that surrounds us today. And yet, like Judy Padilla and so many Rocky Flats employees, we are so soaked in the contamination that we rarely notice it.

This contamination—not only of our planet but also of our

own souls, natures, and relationships—is the toxic end of a chain reaction that started ages ago.

God begins His love letter to us, the Bible, by explaining how our world came to be so polluted. He describes that, given a choice between good and evil, early humans chose evil. The choices of our ancestors ignited an atom-splitting reaction—splitting Adam, Eve, and us away from the perfect existence God desires for us. Ever since, the fallout of evil has continued to spread, infecting our bodies, our nations, even planet Earth itself.

Like Judy Padilla, who lived a normal life—making breakfast for her children, loving her husband, and driving her white 1975 Volkswagen Beetle to work every day—the busyness of life can distract us from the reality that we are living, working, and breathing in a spiritual contamination zone. In fact, the majority of people never do open their eyes to realize the contamination all around them.

To understand why suffering infects our world, we have to understand that we do not live in heaven. We don't even live in the perfect Garden of Eden, where God placed the first humans. We live in a place as polluted as Rocky Flats, a place that started off pure but has become grossly contaminated in every dimension—physically and spiritually.

Too many people of faith skip over the important beginning of the story as God tells it. God, who is loving and good, did not create our world with cancer or death, with divorce, rape, famine, pollution, or weakness. The world that God entrusted to human care had no hunger or pain. God gave that perfect planet, stocked with organic fruits and vegetables, as a gift to early humans. He let them know—*this is important*—that *they* were responsible to care for the planet and its inhabitants.[1]

Then humanity willingly turned away from God and invited evil to occupy the world they were in charge of.[2] With evil came pain, difficulty, and death.

Evil infected a previously perfect planet.[3] Throughout human history, this evil that God calls "sin" has continued spreading, infecting every continent, every country, and every body. This is the infected world we have inherited from our ancestors. None of us are exempt from the fallout of this pollution.

*Trace them back far enough, and the pains and problems in your life today find their roots in this original infection and contamination of humanity.*

If that seems like a lot to swallow, then zoom out from your own pain for a moment. Look around at the world we've been born into. Look at the sickness and hunger in Africa and Haiti. Look at the abuse of women and children in so many countries. Look at the violence and unrest in the Middle East, the pure evil of groups like ISIS, al-Qaeda, and Boko Haram. Look at the human torture and atrocities of World War II.

Consider the reality that 870 million people starve or suffer from malnutrition on a planet that has more than enough food for everyone and more than enough resources to transport that food to the hungry.[4] (That is almost three times the United States population who starve every year.)

Or consider that 768 million people do not have clean drinking water on a planet with more than enough water and more than enough resources to transport that water to the dying.[5] (That's more than twice the U.S. population who are unable today to find clean drinking water.)

Consider that we have drugs to treat and prevent diseases such as malaria, but in 2013, an estimated 584,000 people still died from that disease, even though we have more than enough resources to get the medicine to them.[6] (That is approximately the population of Portland, Oregon, who die every year from easily curable conditions.)

Consider that at least thirteen million orphans today have

neither a mom nor a dad, and many are simply thrown into the grass to die in poor countries, while millions of families with plenty would eagerly care for these children, but organizational barriers stand in the way.[7]

Closer to home, look at the turmoil and discontentment among people living in one of the wealthiest and most comfortable societies in history, the United States. Look at the cold reality that every one of us reading this will breathe a final breath in the next eighty years, much sooner for most of us.

Because of the contamination of evil, we live today in a world where the death rate is 100 percent. From Warren Buffett, Bill Gates, and the world's wealthiest to you and me, none of us get to have a body that won't die on this polluted earth.

Like the shining Rocky Flats facility, our world can look beautiful and productive at first glance, but deeper examination reveals contamination at every level. Like Judy Padilla and thousands of workers, most of us are too busy buzzing about to notice the seeping contamination.

We are broken in our physical bodies and in our relationships. We are also broken in our emotions. Did you know the four most prescribed drugs in the United States are all antidepressants?

The thorn that drove you to read this book provides sharp proof that our world is broken. It's evidence that our world is exactly how God describes it in Scripture—a place as polluted and contaminated as Rocky Flats. Even the weather patterns of earth are broken, often resulting in natural disasters.

Down here in this Rocky Flats world, all of us have weaknesses—no matter how successful, wealthy, talented, or beautiful we are. It's part of the fallout. We've all been contaminated. And it was never supposed to be like this. There was never supposed to be death, pain, or weakness.

God did not build a broken world. He built a perfect world—which evil infected when humans invited evil in.[8]

So if God is really loving and good, then why hasn't He done anything about our pain? Why hasn't He made a way of escape? Why isn't He doing anything to fix what's broken?

Well, it turns out He is.

# CHAPTER 8

# Strength That Is Out of This World

In him was life, and that life was the light of all
mankind. The light shines in the darkness . . .
*John 1:4-5*

*On a Thursday afternoon* in August 2010, thirty-three miners were digging, hauling, and drilling rock deep beneath the Atacama Desert in Chile. A mineshaft above the workers exploded and then collapsed. The thirty-three Chilean miners were trapped in rubble some three miles underground. For about two weeks, the world assumed the men had died.

Then, seventeen days after the collapse, a drill bit returned to the surface with a message taped to it written in bold, red letters: "Estamos bien en el refugio, los 33." (In English, "We are well in the shelter, the 33 of us.")[1]

We are told that "once the rescuers, and the world, knew that the men were alive, Chile implemented a comprehensive plan to both care for the workers during their entrapment and to rescue the miners from the depths."[2]

In the same way, when God looked down and saw humanity trapped in the contaminated rubble of sin, He implemented a two-prong rescue plan—first, to sustain us during our entrapment in this fallen world, and second, to rescue us out of this darkness. This is why Jesus left heaven and came to earth on a rescue operation.

Jesus spoke about this rescue plan when He said that he came that we may have abundant or full life.[3] He came from heaven to give us peace and purpose during our time in this dark world. He also came to rescue us out of the depths entirely. He referred to this escape plan when He said, "My kingdom is not of this world."[4] He didn't come to make Rocky Flats into heaven; He came to light the way *out of* Rocky Flats, to drill to an escape route for you.

This is why Jesus spoke, time and again, of another kingdom, another world—of eternal life. He said, "I am going there to prepare a place for you [and] . . . I will come back and take you to be with me."[5] And "the one who believes in me will live, even though they die."[6]

The government of Chile spent more than twenty million dollars attempting to retrieve those thirty-three miners. It spared no expense.

Does twenty million dollars seem like a lot to spend on thirty-three people? Not if you love the people who need rescue, or especially if you love *one* of them deeply. In the same way, God so valued and so loved *you* that He spared no expense to rescue you. God does not desire for anyone to die in the hopelessness of this contaminated world.[7]

"For God so loved the world that he gave his one and only Son, that whoever believes in him shall not perish but have eternal life."[8]

Whether this is brand-new information or familiar comfort, I wonder, *Have you realized that this is the most basic exchange of God's strength for our weakness?* When we were too weak to rescue ourselves from the contamination of this world, God used His strength to rescue us. This is the most generous exchange of strength for weakness in the history of the universe. Jesus traded paradise for rubble.

The only possible way to rescue you from the fallout of sin was for God Himself to come down into the darkness of humanity in the person of Jesus Christ. As the best firefighters and rescuers do, Jesus gave His own life to rescue those who would otherwise die. He took our death upon Himself.[9]

On October 24, 2010, the rescue of the miners reached its final stage. The thirty-three men had spent sixty-nine days in the fallen mine. They had survived on food and water that was dropped down from above through a three-mile shaft. Those sixty-nine days must have felt like a lifetime, but every minute, every hour, every day, was worth the wait. Because real rescue was coming.

The rescue came in the form of a giant tube, a rescue capsule named the *Fénix* (*Phoenix*). It was a metal cylinder large enough to fit a full-grown man inside. Like a slow-motion bullet, the rescue capsule was threaded down a three-mile tunnel. Then, one at a time, beginning with the sickest and most dehydrated, the miners stepped into the capsule. And, one at a time, they got towed up, still in darkness, through three miles of dirt and rock to the earth's surface.

The men had only one way out of that collapsed mine. A narrow way. But every trapped miner had open access to it.

In the same way, Jesus says, "I am the way and the truth and the life."[10] Yes, His way of rescue is narrow. (Almost every meaningful rescue is.) But Jesus' narrow way of rescue is open and available to everybody. It is open to you.

Choosing to trust Christ as rescuer is the most foundational exchange of your weakness for God's strength.

## Stepping into the Rescue Capsule

Tired, hungry, and dirty, each of those thirty-three miners had to make a choice. When the rescue tube came to them, they had to choose to step into the capsule and get pulled to the top. They had to trust that once they rose one mile up the shaft, the cable wouldn't snap and drop them to their death. By stepping into the rescue capsule, they also admitted their own weakness. They admitted that they could not work their way to the top in their own strength, no matter how hard they tried.

It's the same with God's rescue. Many humans don't realize just how serious our predicament is on earth. But in times of pain and weakness or when watching news of the latest terrorist slaughter of children and innocent civilians, we see through the illusion that this life is heaven.

Through Christ, the path to the top is open to everybody. But accepting God's rescue requires us to abandon our own efforts to save ourselves. It requires us to take a step of faith into His strength. It requires trust.

We begin by *admitting* that, like every other human being, *we are infected with evil and sin*. We've all had embarrassing impulses that we've willed into action. We are all born into a world of sin. Our contamination separates all of us spiritually from a perfect God.

"All have sinned and fall short of the glory of God."[11]

The writer Oswald Chambers put it this way: "If I know I have no strength of will, no nobility of disposition, then Jesus says— 'Blessed are you,' because it is through this poverty that I enter His kingdom. I cannot enter His kingdom as a good man or woman; I can only enter it as a complete pauper."[12] Our thorns, pains, and weaknesses remind us that we are paupers. There are things in our lives beyond our control, and we need God's help.

Evil covered our world in darkness. Jesus came as a light into that oily darkness, to bring Good News. Great rescues require radical sacrifice. Christ's rescue of us required His sacrifice and death on the cross. He took the penalty of our mistakes upon Himself so we could escape from the contamination of this polluted world.

Just as those miners had to decide whether or not to trust in the *Fénix* rescue capsule, each of us must decide whether or not we trust in God's rescue. We trust by *believing that Jesus died on the cross for our mistakes and sins.*

"God demonstrates his own love in this: While we were still sinners, Christ died for us."[13]

Like the miners who left behind the darkness of that collapsed mine, *we choose to step into the life God offers and turn away from the life controlled by fear, death, and evil.* Like the early humans who turned away from God and chose evil, we have a choice that only we can make.

Our choice: turn away from evil and back toward God, or continue living under the darkness of a collapsed world. Only you can choose for yourself:

- a life contaminated by the pollution of evil, defined by your weakness

or

- a life of God's forgiveness and rescue, defined by His strength

The choice is yours. In fact, you might even circle (or highlight if using an e-reader) which of the two you choose today. If you choose the second, then *tell God that you want Jesus to call the shots in your life.* Tell Him you want to turn away from yourself and from your way of doing things—to trust His rescue instead. Scripture says that "if you declare with your mouth, 'Jesus is Lord,' and believe in your heart that God raised him from the dead, you will be saved."[14]

The Chilean miners didn't have to understand every detail of their rescue in order to set foot in the *Fénix* rescue capsule. In the same way, you don't have to answer every question about creation, Scripture, or Christianity in order to simply place your faith in the cross and thus step into Jesus Christ's rescue.

The moment you reach out to God, believing that Jesus died on the cross to reach you, you receive God's free gift of rescue. Despite what many religious people say, God tells us that forgiveness and eternal life in heaven are *free gifts* to be accepted. We cannot earn them any more than a trapped miner could have worked his way up to the surface through three miles of solid rock.

"For the wages of sin is death, but the gift of God is eternal life in Christ Jesus our Lord."[15]

When Jesus rose from the dead (after His execution on the cross), He proved He has the power to move freely between the afterlife and this life. Between heaven and earth. He is God over time and humanity. He has the power to defeat death and the power to move us from the collapsed mineshaft to the surface—from Rocky Flats to heaven. He promises that "everyone who calls on the name of the Lord will be saved."[16]

Remember the note in red letters that came up on the drill bit, saying there were thirty-three men alive in the collapsed mine? In John 3, we find another note in red letters:

> For God so loved the world that he gave his one and only Son, that whoever believes in him shall . . . have eternal life. For God did not send his Son into the world to condemn the world, but to save the world through him. Whoever believes in him is not condemned, but whoever does not believe stands condemned already . . .

Because of a great collapse, those thirty-three miners were condemned to death until rescue came their way. Because of the great collapse of sin, all humanity is trapped and condemned to death. But rescue has come our way. Jesus came down into our world on a rescue mission that He knew would cost Him His life. At the cross, He provided escape for you and me. He provided the strength of heaven for the greatest weakness on earth.

By the way, this reality—the spiritual contamination of the Rocky Flats world we live in—is the reason that so many hopes prove to be empty and false in this life. A new job in Rocky Flats, a new spouse in Rocky Flats, a new car or medical treatment in Rocky Flats, a new anything in Rocky Flats, can't give real hope, because it's all contaminated. Only Jesus gives a hope that delivers us out of this world.

One morning after Jesus' death, people came to His grave looking for His corpse. They couldn't find it. Jesus had risen from the dead, proving He is Almighty God, showing He can move freely between heaven and earth. Those searching for Jesus' body were greeted with this question: "Why do you look for the living among the dead?"[17]

Most of us spend our lives looking for *living hope* among *dead* things. We scour the rubble of a collapsed mineshaft, a Rocky Flats world, expecting to find heaven. All hopes down here prove, eventually, to be imperfect. If you don't believe that, look at the hopeless deaths of Michael Jackson, Whitney Houston, Heath Ledger, Philip Seymour Hoffman, Robin Williams, Howard Hughes, and Marilyn Monroe—people who tasted, owned, and investigated every available pleasure and hope that Rocky Flats has to offer.

If the divorces, suicides, and overdoses of the world's richest, most talented, and most famous are any indication, this world's hopes are as empty as God says they are. We need a different kind of hope, one that lifts us out of the darkness.

Jesus didn't come to peddle another false hope in the contamination of Rocky Flats. He drilled down into our world to provide a way out. That's the hope of Jesus—hope that the escape tunnel has been carved into the flesh of the universe.

As we begin trusting Jesus' way of escape, we immediately begin to see His power, restoration, and rescue at work in our own weaknesses. We begin to experience the strength of heaven for our life on earth, sustaining us for our brief time in Rocky Flats.

God's strength in your weakness rises or falls on this crucial choice:

- a life of self-weakness in the darkness

or

- a life of God's strength in the light, by believing in Christ

For your soul, for your strength and your eternity, it's a choice only you can make.

# CHAPTER 9

# *Already/Not Yet Strength*

If we enter the narrow road, it will be rocky
and rough and tough. But at the end is
heaven. And while on that road, there's
a new resource and a new power and a
new joy and a new love that God gives.

*Billy Graham*

My *son Jack* ran up to me the other day, jumping up and down, shouting, "Dad, Dad, I found a hair on my arm!"

This is a big moment for a young boy. I examined, and sure enough, there was a tiny, clear hair on his arm.

"Way to go, Jack," I told him. "As you grow bigger, you'll get lots more hairs on both your arms."

Jack replied, "But I already am bigger, and I already have hairs."

Me: "What I mean, Jack, is that someday you'll be as tall as I am."

Jack: "But I already am tall, Daddy."

It's true that at thirty-four pounds and about three feet tall, Jack is a lot taller and heavier than he was as a newborn. Of course, it's also true that he will continue to get much taller and heavier as he continues growing.

Since his birth, Jack has "already" gained twenty-five pounds, but he will continue gaining another 125 or more if he remains healthy. He has "already" grown about sixteen inches taller, but he will continue growing twice as tall.

Jack has "already" grown, but he is "not yet" fully grown. And that's just as true of our spiritual growth as it is of Jack's physical growth. Theologians call this the "already/not yet."

The moment we trust in Christ to rescue us from sin, we are "already" adopted into God's family. But we are "not yet" home in heaven, where there will be no more pain or weakness. We are "already" purified from the fallout of sin *internally* in our souls, but we are "not yet" out of these broken bodies that feel pain, have broken emotions, and will eventually die in Rocky Flats.

The day is coming (after our time on earth) when from heaven we will see fully the rescue we "already" have. Until then, we journey through this contaminated world, growing every day. Just like Jack's physical growth, our rescue is "already/not yet." We are "already" purified internally, but we are "not yet" at home in heaven. We are new creations in an old world.

What does this mean for you and your weaknesses? It means the day is coming when God will "wipe every tear" from your eye (Revelation 21:4). The day is coming when Joy Veron (the paralyzed mother from chapter 1) will not need a wheelchair. The day is coming when I will not have to worry about a hemiplegic episode turning into a stroke—because I won't have any hemiplegic episodes at all. The day is coming when all who trust Christ's rescue will be entirely free from pain, sickness, and weakness.

But when we look around us, it's clear that day is "not yet" fully here. Even the strongest and most spiritual people still battle through weakness, doubt, prisons, sickness, death, and depression in this world—just as Paul the apostle did. God acknowledges this tension—that Christ has "already" defeated death, but has "not yet" kicked all evil out of planet Earth. After declaring that all things are under Christ's control, Scripture adds, "Yet at present we do not see everything subject" to Christ.[1]

And so we might wonder, *Does trusting Christ's rescue make any difference for my difficulties right here and now?* The answer is a resounding yes. Trusting Christ makes a life-changing difference for your journey through this contaminated world.

Just as much as Christ promises our eternal rescue, He also promises to sustain us on earth while we await that rescue. Writer Paul David Tripp put it like this: "The promise of future grace always carries with it the promise of present grace."[2]

Remember the trapped Chilean miners? The rescue operation had two halves: (1) to *rescue* them out of the collapsed mineshaft and (2) to *sustain* them with food, water, and medical supplies until they got pulled up to the surface.

God's plan for us works the same way. The good news of Christ is not only that He is delivering us out of our prisons in this world (eternal life in heaven), but also that He will sustain and strengthen us while we live down here (abundant life).

When your suffering discourages you, your soul is groaning for heaven. When you feel internally unsettled by the evils, injustices, and tragedies of this world, your inner being is homesick, longing to be where you belong—a place free from suffering and heartbreak.

God promises us this pain-free future, far better than any good we can imagine: "Then I saw a new heaven and a new earth . . . He will wipe every tear from their eyes. There will be no more death or mourning or crying or pain, for the old order of things has passed away."[3]

The "old order of things" that will pass away is the contamination of Rocky Flats. Until then, Christ promises to sustain and strengthen you on your journey to heaven. Every weakness reminds you that you are "not yet" home. And every weakness also provides an opportunity to discover that in Christ you "already" have the power of heaven available to sustain you in the darkness of earth.

God promises to give you the strength you need to live for Him as you await heaven: "His divine power has given us everything we need for a godly life."[4]

Just as much as Christ will rescue you *out of this world* into heaven, He will also sustain and strengthen you with heaven's power *in this world*.

## God over Life's Storms

> No power on earth or in hell can conquer
> the Spirit of God living within the human
> spirit; it creates an inner invincibility.
>
> *Oswald Chambers*

I saw some great thunderstorms growing up in Michigan, but Arizona's monsoons have a unique magnificence all their own. When I first moved to Arizona, I would drive out into a valley during monsoon thunderstorms. I would watch the blinding bursts of lightning stabbing at the bowl of mountains encircling me. It was all storm, in every direction. (Disclaimer: I do not recommend this.)

In life, we sometimes find ourselves surrounded by storms. As a pastor, I've walked with friends through some of the most frightening storms imaginable. Unexpected death. Life-changing accidents. Cancer. Infidelity. Heart-crushing relapses into addiction. Natural disasters. Slander and media misrepresentation.

I wonder what storms you've found yourself in recently?

- the storm of death
- the storm of inadequacy
- the storm of illness
- the storm of rejection
- the storm of addiction

- the storm of anxiety
- the storm of fatigue
- the storm of decisions
- the storm of opposition and persecution
- the storm of aging
- the storm of loneliness

This Rocky Flats world swarms with frightening storms. When we are in them, it can seem like these storms will never end. It can seem like God has forgotten us and has forgotten about the rescue plan.

God wants you to know He has not forgotten you. He has not abandoned you in your storm. He has "already" begun the process of rescuing you out of your storms, even when it does not feel like it. Even though you're "not yet" in the safety and calm of heaven.

My best friend is an airplane pilot. After he earned his private pilot license, he would take me up for flights in a small propeller-driven Piper airplane. One day, we encountered heavy turbulence. The tiny plane began convulsing, bouncing, and shaking. When I looked out the window and saw the wing flexing up and down, I was sure the whole wing was going to break off.

My friend the pilot seemed unconcerned. "The turbulence is from a storm," he said. "All we have to do is get above the clouds." For the next few minutes, we flew straight into the very clouds that were causing the commotion, wings bouncing, seats rattling, hearts thumping (mine anyway).

Then after a few moments, we popped out on top of the clouds. It was like watching a sunrise. Suddenly the sky above was clear blue. Beams of sunlight stretched out in every direction. It was calm. And best of all, the wings stopped flapping.

The storm had not gone away; we had simply risen above it.

This is God's promise for you while you wait for your complete deliverance out of this world. Like everyone else in Rocky Flats, believers in Christ still endure storms. God does not always give "get out of jail free" cards to His people. (If He did, how much could we relate to the hurting people we are here to help? Jesus related to our pain, and now, for a brief season, we who follow Him continue sharing in the pains of the people He calls us to help.)

God may not calm the storms of your circumstances, but He will lift you high above them—if you will let Him fly you *into* the clouds. Most folks never get above the clouds, though, because they refuse to fly directly into the source of turbulence.

If you do allow God to lead you into your storm clouds, you will eventually find yourself atop the darkness. We saw this with Joy Veron, the paralyzed mom. Her broken back and legs are "not yet" healed in this Rocky Flats world, but Joy is "already" experiencing heaven's strength for her life on earth.

Joy could have chosen to spend the rest of her days on earth pouting because God has not miraculously healed her paralysis (Isn't that what we often do with our storms—demand that God still them and pout if He doesn't?). Instead, Joy let God fly her straight into the clouds. Now God is carrying Joy above the storm of paralysis—giving her a peace and contentment that rise above the circumstances of her life.

God can carry you above your storms too. Jesus tells us, "In this world you will have trouble." Jesus then promises to carry us above the troubles: "But take heart! I have overcome the world."[5] Trouble will come into all our lives in this contaminated, Rocky Flats world. But that trouble doesn't have to overwhelm or overcome the person who trusts Christ.

The prophet Isaiah warned that, no matter how strong any of us are, we will encounter storms that weaken and even topple us. "Even youths grow tired and weary, and young men stumble and fall," he wrote. "But those who hope in the LORD will renew their strength. They will soar on wings like eagles."[6]

That word *hope* is a Hebrew word. It means "to trust" and "to wait." And so "those who *trust* in the LORD will renew their strength." And "those who *wait* on the LORD will renew their strength."

*Trust* means being sure God will sustain me. He will never abandon me.

*Wait* means a stubborn hope, a confidence that this storm is not the end for me.

Because we occupy a fallen world, we will face some difficulties that won't miraculously or immediately improve (as Paul's thorn did not). When we find ourselves in such storms, it does us no good to fixate on changing the difficult circumstances. Instead, we can fix our hope on Christ, who will both carry us above the circumstances and also carry us to heaven. Christ, who has "already" started our "not yet" completed rescue.[7]

In 1915, a gifted young artist and teacher named Oswald Chambers volunteered to be a chaplain for British soldiers in Egypt during World War I. Chambers knew what it was to trust God through the pains of life. He died in Egypt, at the age of forty-two, from untreated appendicitis.

Chambers's wife compiled his sermons into a devotional book titled *My Utmost for His Highest*. Through this book, Chambers continues to strengthen millions of people.

Through Chambers's weakness, the strength of God emerged. Chambers had learned that the deepest joy in life, *spiritual* joy, does not grow into us from outward circumstances. Rather, it grows outward from *within* the soul connected to Christ by faith. He put it this way:

Where do the saints get their joy? . . . We might think from just observing them that they have no burdens at all to bear. But we must lift the veil from our eyes. The fact that the peace, light, and joy of God is in them is proof that a burden is there as well. The burden . . . squeezes the grapes in our lives and produces the wine, but most of us see only the wine and not the burden. No power on earth or in hell can conquer the Spirit of God living within the human spirit; it creates an inner invincibility.[8]

God can lift you up above the storms of your life. As you find God's strength in and through your weakness, it will change your life. God can transform your weakness from a problem to a power outlet, from a stumbling block to a springboard.

Just as you can take a nap in the tension of a physical hammock, so your soul can rest in the tension of this "already/not yet" rescue. Paul writes that the peace of God, which goes beyond all understanding, is *already* available. It will guard your heart and your mind as you await complete deliverance and rescue.[9]

Even when you feel like heaven is so far away. Even when it feels as though you're moving *away from* heaven's freedom instead of *toward* it. Even when it seems like the troubles of this world may overwhelm you, may overtake us all.

When that happens, remember my young son. Remember Jack, jumping up and down, shouting, "Dad, Dad, I found a hair on my arm!"

At thirty-four pounds, Jack is "already/not yet" grown.

And impaled with our thorns, we are "already/not yet" home.

# PART 4

# HOPEFUL SONGS IN A GLORIOUS RUIN

*The Window of Hope*

# CHAPTER 10

# Trading Limits for Limitless

---

So we fix our eyes not on what is seen, but
on what is unseen, since what is seen is
temporary, but what is unseen is eternal.

*2 Corinthians 4:18*

*The five Great Lakes* hold 20 percent of the world's fresh water. These are not ponds. They are oceanic in size—and the water they hold is cool, drinkable, and life-giving.

While in high school, some friends and I took a day trip to one of these Great Lakes—Lake Michigan. We had heard about a sand dune, a small desert of soft beach sand that rolled on and on, eventually tumbling down to a scenic shore and remote stretch of waterfront.

We decided to walk through the sand dune toward the lake. After a three-hour drive, we arrived at a park with a sign that mapped the way. We set off with a few coolers of food and a whole bunch of energy.

Patches of grass poked through the sand when we began. Slowly the grass disappeared, giving way to the sand. If someone dropped you in that very spot, you might think you had landed in the vast Sahara or in Death Valley. But in fact, we stood less than one mile from the largest supply of fresh water in the world.

The sand dunes were a spilling stack of hills and mounds, sculpted by wind and time. Each time we saw the top of a hill, we imagined Lake Michigan on the other side. And time after time, we would crest another hill, only to find more sand stretching out before us.

Some hills were small, just ten or fifteen feet high. Others seemed like mountains, with little hills freckled across them. Carried along by a great hope that the lake lay over there somewhere, we kept heading west.

The soft sand slowed our steps, and our legs grew tired. But we trudged along. After ten or fifteen minutes, it started to get hot. We grew thirsty. And some from our little group began doubting that we were still heading in the right direction.

Just when we all suspected this was indeed the Sahara—that we had been fooled, lied to, deceived in our faith—just then, a report echoed back from the front of the group.

"Water!" the shout ricocheted back to us.

We lifted our heavy feet and made a run for it.

It's quite a moment when you crest over the top of that final ridge. So many times, you have peaked over another sandy ledge, only to find more sand. But this time you rise over the edge to find a vast sea of cool, refreshing water. It laps against the sand in constant waves, small frothy whitecaps dancing on the midnight blue.

The water—cold, diamond-sparkling under the sun, and thirst quenching—grows out further than you can see to the right, to the left, and so far out into the distance that no islands or land interrupt the horizon. Just cool, fresh, salt-free water. So clear that, on that sunny day, we could venture waist-deep in it and still see our toes wiggling below in the sand.

Fresh water. And more of it than anywhere else in the world.

In many ways, that journey through the dunes parallels our journey through this life on earth. It sometimes seems like we'll never arrive in God's Promised Land, where He will reunite us with lost loved ones, where He will heal our pains and illnesses once and for all, where every thirst will find satisfaction in His life-giving presence.

Our journey sometimes seems so dry and hopeless. We wrestle with the temptation to give up on our faith that something greater awaits us over the hills. Our legs strain under the weight. We crest yet another hill to find, once again, more sand on the other side. And we wonder if the promises of Jesus are true.

One of the great forgotten themes of Scripture is that God calls His believers "strangers," "pilgrims," "foreigners," and "travelers." Peter the apostle got this. He wrote a book to struggling and hurting believers. He did not encourage them that everything in their life circumstances would improve—if only they had enough faith.

Instead, he encouraged them that everything here is temporary. He wrote, "Set your hope fully on the grace that will be brought to you at the revelation [appearing] of Jesus Christ."[1]

My friends and I kept trudging through those dunes, not because we thought the burning sand was beautiful or comfortable, but because we had set our hope fully on Lake Michigan.

Peter says that you can choose to "set your hope"—and not only to set it but to set it "fully." We can choose to place our hope in Christ rather than in the shifting sands of circumstance.

We are "foreigners here" in a world where Satan has control over many of the earth's strategic resources.[2] We are making our way to a better land, with "an inheritance that can never perish, spoil or fade."[3] And while we make our way through the dunes of this life, we are "shielded by God's power until the coming of the salvation that is ready to be revealed in the last time."[4]

We can find joy in the midst of our difficulty by fixing our hope and our eyes on the future deliverance we have in Christ: "In all this you greatly rejoice, though now for a little while you may have had to suffer grief in all kinds of trials."[5]

We continue clinging to our faith. We cling all the tighter as the suffering increases. We continue choosing God in the burning desert sands of life, trusting that He is leading us to the water. When we do that, our perseverance refines our eternal inner being, just as gold is refined by being melted down and then cooled.[6]

From Genesis to Revelation, God's people in Scripture acknowledged that this world was not their home. Somehow many of us have lost that way of seeing reality. Maybe because we live in a wealthy society. Maybe because the people around tell us and assume that this world is it, the best it will get, home *and* heaven.

But God encourages us to live like we're headed to a better place. This world is not our heaven, our hope, or our home. We are making our way through the dunes of earth toward a better land with God.

Paul the apostle called his thorn in the flesh a gift. When our thorns shake us enough to wake us from our self-satisfied slumber, when our thorns force us to realize that this world is not our home, then those thorns have become gifts.

———

> I was given the gift of a handicap to
> keep me in constant touch with my
> limitations . . . At first I didn't think of it as
> a gift, and begged God to remove it.
> *2 Corinthians 12:7-8 MSG*

The life-giving waters of Lake Michigan offer us another lesson. My lakeward trudge led to a place where the dunes ended and the water began. It's a lot like the place where our own limits end and God's limitlessness begins.

Right now, in our time on earth, we can either live in the dunes of our own strength or we can make our way toward the limitless strength of God. Christians who do not have thorns in their lives (or who do not recognize their thorns for what they are) rarely move out of the dunes of Christian living. They rarely reach the boundaries of their own capability and comfort.

I did not embark on a study of Paul's "thorn in the flesh" because I was curious. My pain and suffering drove me to study the "thorn in the flesh." In the process, I've discovered a strength I never knew I had when I lived a more comfortable life.

I have now spent a few years studying Paul's thorn, reading his description of it over and over, rereading the letter of 2 Corinthians in multiple translations and in its original language, and studying various commentaries about the text.

At one point, after months of study, I remained baffled by Paul's claim that he "delights" in weaknesses, pains, insults, and thorns.[7] I understood what he meant as an idea or theory. But I wanted more. I wanted to experience it as a reality in my own pains.

One day, while praying that God would move me through this gateway to heaven's strength, I finally grasped Paul's big point in 2 Corinthians 12. Here it is:

*Where your limits dead-end, God's limitlessness begins.*

This is what Paul was getting at when he wrote, "I was given the gift of a handicap to keep me in constant touch with my limitations . . . At first I didn't think of it as a gift, and begged God to remove it."

After Paul asked God to remove the thorn of pain, God told him "My grace is sufficient for you, for my power is made perfect in weakness."[8] Paul then says that *because* of his thorn—*because* of it—Christ's power pulsed even more through his life.

In other words, Paul says that his thorn pushed him out of the sand dunes. His pain pushed him beyond himself to a place where he could experience the strength of God's limitlessness. Afterward, Paul realized he never would have moved beyond his own capabilities had he not had a thorn that would push him beyond himself.

Paul is talking about moving past the boundary of his own capabilities, past the dunes, and there discovering God's limitless capability.

*Where your limits dead-end, God's limitlessness begins.*

If my friends and I had given up in the sand, we never would have experienced Lake Michigan. Many Christians live their entire lives in the sand of their own limitations, getting as much pleasure, comfort, and security as they can find within the boundaries of their limited human capacity and comfort.

God is teaching us that our thorns, our pains, and our disappointments can prod us past the edges of our own capability.

If not for pain, many of us reading this book would not be seeking God's strength in our lives right now. Instead, we would feel quite happy to remain in the sand of our own desires, abilities, plans, pleasures, families, retirements, or careers. But when we choose to step out beyond the boundary of our own capabilities, when we pass that border, that's when we discover the great freshwater sea of God's limitlessness.

Even Paul, having seen Christ face-to-face, having performed miracles—even he would have settled for a comfortable life in the dunes of his own limitations had God not allowed "the gift" of weakness to drive Paul beyond his own limitations. Because of this gift, Paul moved beyond his limits and learned to swim in the limitless power of God.

Horrendous as our thorns in the flesh are, they have potential to become the agents that drive us out of the dunes of self-dependence. This is why Paul, as he looked back, could call his thorn a "gift." If we will continue seeking God, our pains can drive us, hill after hill, ridge after ridge, toward the great, unlimited supply of God's strength, refreshment, and living water for our lives.

I pray that in your inner being, the place accessible only to you and God, you keep choosing to move beyond your limits toward the Limitless One. I pray that in your inner being, you keep stepping toward the refreshing, life-giving water.

God knows your pain. And He does have plans, as you trust in Him, to fully heal you of your pain, to fully restore you and redeem whatever you have lost. Until then, you can journey toward His strength with great hope.

With each step forward,

> we trade our limits for His limitless;
> we trade our inability for His capability;
> we exchange our pain for His healing,
> our weakness for heaven's strength.

Day by day, we clear hill after hill on our way to that place where our limits and sufferings end.

And ahead, a great cloud of witnesses has gone before.[9] Sometimes, if I listen closely, I think I hear their shouts of joy echoing back this way.

"Water!"

CHAPTER 11

# Smiling through Tears

Instead of trusting in our own strength
or wits to get out of it, we were
forced to trust God totally . . .
*Paul the apostle, 2 Corinthians 1:9-10 MSG*

*At age four,* I was thrust into a T-ball league. I watched the action
from underneath a size XL navy blue baseball cap.

T-ball is the putt-putt version of baseball, in which kids hit a
large stationary ball off the top of a rubber tee. Or in my case, it
was the sport in which I hit the rubber tee, and the ball fell off,
thumping to the ground.

After a few outfield incidents (in which I was literally picking
dandelions), I took an early retirement, ending what could have
been a long and an embarrassing baseball career.

What I lack in athletic ability, however, I make up for in nerd-
ability. I don't know *how* to hit a home run in baseball. But I know
a bit about the physics that make it happen. I know that, for a
batter to hit a home run, a handful of ingredients must converge
at the same time—in precisely the right spot.

Athletes and trainers call this "the sweet spot." It's a physical
place on the baseball bat, measuring only about an inch in length.

When the pitcher throws the baseball, it hurtles toward the
batter, spinning and arcing at 88 to 103 miles per hour. That is fast
enough to kill you—if the ball hits you in the head, as happened
to Major League batter Ray Chapman. On August 16, 1920, a New

York Yankees pitcher threw a fastball into Chapman's skull. He died twelve hours later.

Your challenge as a batter is not only to hit the lethally quick baseball but also to strike the ball with the one-inch sweet spot on the bat. Depending on how the pitcher threw it, the ball may be curving, sliding, or still as a rock as it splits the air, creating an audible wake of wind just inches from your nose.

When a swinging batter successfully connects the sweet spot on the bat to the bulleting ball, a home run happens. It doesn't matter if the pitch is a curveball. It doesn't matter if the pitcher is a lefty southpaw. It doesn't matter if it's raining or shining. Connect the sweet spot of the bat to the baseball, and that ball is headed over the fence.

The sweet spot is so important that some professionals train with bats that have a diamond-shaped sweet spot painted on the bat. They watch video footage and adjust their stance or grip to better contact the sweet spot.

Major League Baseball generates seven billion dollars per year. All that money comes down to this one tiny piece of real estate smaller than one inch in length—the sweet spot.

The trials of your life create a sweet spot too. It is the intersection of the difficulties thrown at you and how you connect with them.

The majority of us cannot hit the sweet spot of the baseball bat on a ninety-mile-per-hour pitch. (Even the pros fail half the time.) In the same way, we all face difficulties in life that we are incapable of turning into anything good in our own strength.

When life throws us a devastating fastball of tragedy, we can only hit the sweet spot by placing our lives into God's more capable hands. One of God's important messages in the Bible is that when life throws you evil, *He* has the ability to hit the sweet spot and turn your tragedies into victories.

With the easier difficulties of life, the slow pitches, sometimes we can hit the sweet spot in our own strength. Enough positive thinking, a good attitude—and we hit a home run, turning our smaller tragedies into triumphs.

But at other times, life throws more at us than we can handle. A fastball of suffering knocks us down to the ground. Then comes another. And another. Paralyzing pain. Unexpected tragedy. Death. Cancer. Just when we start to get our life back together, in comes another fastball. Enough of these—and we crawl into a life of surviving.

Eventually, we face a fastball of tragedy that we, in ourselves, do not have the strength to turn into victory. Our posture and stance are not perfect. Our grip on life fails.

The bat bounces to the ground. And we huddle there in the dirt, hoping to survive.

That's probably how Joseph felt, when his older brothers threw him in a pit and abandoned him in the wilderness. Angry and jealous, they left Joseph to die, to bake in the Middle Eastern sun.

While Joseph struggled at the bottom of the pit, one of his brothers saw dust rising on the horizon. It signaled a roving band of slave traders, making their way toward Egypt.

"Hey, why leave Joseph to die? We could sell him and make a buck on the deal!"[1]

Sell him they did.

Joseph's life went from security in a large family and favored by his dad to chains that dug into his flesh as he limped mile after mile on feet that blistered from the restless pace. Slave drivers whipped him when he couldn't keep up, prodding, shoving, and shouting.

(God included this true story in the Bible because, among other reasons, it sounds a lot like how Satan has treated God's favored creation—humans. We have been sold into the slavery of sin, but God has the power to turn even that evil for good, as

Joseph's life demonstrates. And God can turn the unthinkable evil in your life for good as well.)

Joseph found himself surrounded by other slaves. Some were frighteningly strong. Others were frighteningly wounded from beatings delivered by their traffickers. Others coughed up blood, wheezed, or shuffled along behind the slave cart, their bodies giving out under the strain.

In what ways can you relate to Joseph?

Betrayed by family or trusted friends?

Emotionally wounded?

Left for dead?

Used and profited from?

Physically aching?

Hungry?

Alone?

Confused by an unthinkable twist in events?

Here Joseph found himself. Not only sold into slavery, but sold as a Hebrew speaker to Midianite and Ishmaelite slave traders, unable to understand the shouts of his captors. They dragged, pushed, and whipped him on a forced march to the slave market in Egypt.

*Talk about life throwing you a paralyzing evil that you cannot possibly turn into good!*

Joseph found himself an owned slave with no legal rights—purchased property, belonging to an Egyptian master.

How could any good come from *this* fastball of suffering?

How could there even be a sweet spot to bring good out of this tragedy?

Physically, Joseph ached, his back notched up and bleeding from the slaver's whip.

Emotionally, Joseph carried wounds deep within him, inflicted by relatives who should have protected him but instead betrayed him.

Relationally, Joseph struggled as a slave to adapt to a foreign culture.

Spiritually, Joseph must have wondered how God could possibly be good and trustworthy.

Somehow Joseph did choose to trust God. He put his life into God's hands, and in time, God hit the sweet spot, giving Joseph favor with his Egyptian owner. In time, Joseph became right-hand man to a wealthy Egyptian. Joseph remained a slave, but he was respected. He managed his master's entire estate.

Then another unthinkable injustice took place. Joseph was falsely accused, lied about, and thrown into prison.

Do you ever feel like you've endured the worst that life could throw at you—only to discover that life had *even more suffering* to throw your way? Joseph must have felt this way. After overcoming those impossible odds and settling into a comfortable, rewarding life, Joseph got betrayed again.

He found himself imprisoned. The metal chains digging into the familiar old ruts of flesh on his wrists and ankles. Just when those old wounds were beginning to heal, Joseph got thrown down again.

Somehow Joseph continued choosing to set his life back into God's hands, fastball after fastball. Somehow, he kept believing that God is big enough and strong enough to repurpose pain and suffering.

And that's what God did.

After years of struggle and years of trusting God to work good from his pain, Joseph became right-hand man to the pharaoh of Egypt. What Joseph could not do on his own—bring good out of his pain—God did, because Joseph handed his life to God. (You can read the entire story, with all the dramatic ups and downs, in Genesis 37–50.)

After years of suffering physical and emotional pain, Joseph became the second most powerful person in the world. He lived a life of unparalleled luxury, purpose, and power. But this did not happen immediately. In the pit, in the slave house, in the prison, all along, Joseph kept turning to God in faith when life threw him one curveball after another.

Just as we have to journey through our own difficulties, Joseph had to journey through betrayal, slavery, beatings, prisons, language barriers, abuse, physical wounds, emotional wounds, lies, rejection, and failure. Any and every thorn we can imagine, Joseph carried it around in the flesh of his soul.

And yet at the end of his life, when he reunited with those brothers who had sold him into slavery, he smiled through tears and told them, "You meant evil against me, but God meant it for good."[2]

The evil they threw into Joseph's life—fastballs of injustice—God had repurposed for good. Why? Because Joseph continually set his life into God's strong, capable hands.

This is the sweet spot of surrender—a stubborn belief that, impossible as it seems, God can repurpose good out of the evil thrown at us. The God who recycles winter into spring every year can also recycle the pain and death in our lives, if only we will set our lives into His hands.

Theologians have a nickname for this miracle. They call it redemption. From our prisons of pain, from our present winter, we can lift our eyes, look out the window, and squint toward the future spring when God will raise the dead things to life. When He will turn all the evil in our lives for good. This is the hope of redemption—a stubborn belief that God will repurpose our pain for good through Christ.

———

When difficulty rushes into our lives, we have only two choices available to us: turn away from God because of the pain or turn toward God with the pain, handing it to Him.

When we turn *toward* God with our pain, He has the power to turn that evil, hurt, or harm into good, repurposing it, redeeming it.

Conversely, when we cling to the hurt ourselves, when we believe the lie that God does not care about us, that we can handle our difficulty better than He can, we unwittingly turn away from the only One in the universe who has the power to repurpose our evil for good.

Paul the apostle experienced this choice with his thorn in the flesh, just as you experience it with yours. He wrote this to some believers who made the choice to turn *toward* God when life threw them problems and pain: "You let the distress bring you to God, not drive you from him. The result was all gain, no loss."[3]

"Distress that drives us to God," Paul writes, "turns us around. It gets us back in the way of salvation. We never regret that kind of pain. But those who let distress drive them away from God are full of regrets, end up on a deathbed of regrets."[4]

Whether your pain drives you *toward* God or *away* from God does not depend on your pain; it depends on you. Turn toward God with your pain, and in time, you will see Him repurpose the evil in your life for good. Keep setting your life in His hands, and you'll find yourself identifying with these words: "And now, isn't it wonderful all the ways in which this distress has goaded you closer to God? You're more alive, more concerned, more sensitive, more reverent, more human, more passionate, more responsible."[5]

In boxing, they say, "The bigger they are, the harder they fall." The baseball equivalent is, "The faster they are, the further they fly." When the sweet spot on the bat connects with the baseball, all the energy of the hurtling ball is redirected and repurposed to achieve a home run. So the frighteningly fast pitch is actually the *preferred* pitch.

A one-hundred-mile-per-hour fastball would frighten most of us if it rushed by, inches from our nose. But for a skilled batter, the faster the fastball, the better. *Faster is better because all that negative energy will be transferred into positive energy when it connects with the sweet spot.*

That's what God did in Joseph's life. Others threw evil at Joseph. Impossibly fast evil that Joseph could never absorb or make into anything good. But God had the strength to transfer that massive negative energy into something massively positive.

And so Joseph, reflecting on his life, realized that what others had thrown at him to harm him, God had repurposed to help him. Not only that, but God *amplified* the good, making the story bigger than Joseph. God repurposed the evil in Joseph's life to save Joseph's family from starvation. (A great famine had left them malnourished and dying, but Joseph controlled the largest food stockpile in the world—Pharaoh's.) God's repurposing in Joseph's life also rescued Jesus' ancestors so that *all* believers could be redeemed and repurposed in Christ.

God recorded the story of Joseph because it gives us a small picture (like every winter and spring) of the redemption He is in the process of working for all who call out to Him. This is the sort of repurposing He is waiting to do for you when you set your difficulty into His hands.

Whatever is being thrown at you, God is capable of connecting that negative energy with the sweet spot and sending it hurtling away from you in positive ways.

When the pain seems unbearable, I remind myself that the faster the pitch, the bigger the hit. The more painful it is now, the more beautiful it will be when I see God miraculously turn the pain for good. I might see it in this life, or I might not see it until the next life.

For believers who keep hoping in heaven, God promises, "No

eye has seen, no ear has heard, and no mind has imagined what God has prepared for those who love him."[6]

The day is coming, soon, when God will unveil how He has been working in all things "for the good of those who love him."[7]

Of that promise, Rick Warren writes these words:

The events in your life work *together* in God's plan. They are not isolated acts, but interdependent parts of the process to make you like Christ. To bake a cake you must use flour, salt, raw eggs, sugar, and oil. Eaten individually, each is pretty distasteful or even bitter. But bake them together and they become delicious. If you will give God all your distasteful, unpleasant experiences, he will blend them together for good.[8]

Warren goes on to write: "This does not say that everything in life is good. Much of what happens in our world is evil and bad, but God specializes in bringing good out of it."[9]

*The more painful it is now, the more beautiful it will be when we see God miraculously turn the pain for good.*

Like most of us, Joseph would have preferred a pain-free life. But as pain exploded into his world, Joseph continually surrendered his life into God's capable hands, opening the way for God to repurpose unthinkable evil into unimaginable good.

This great repurposing culminated when Joseph, because of his authority in Egypt, saved the lives of the very brothers who had betrayed him.

When Joseph reunited with his family, emotion overcame him.[10] A tight throat and watery eyes gave way to heaving sobs. Joseph cried as he remembered the bitter pain, as he recalled the slave master's whip, the winding and difficult journey to joy.

Through teary eyes, Joseph saw how God had repurposed all that evil into something sweet, good, and life-saving.

Joseph saw that God had, all along, been working to turn the evil of a fallen earth for the good of His believers, declaring that "it was to save lives that God sent me ahead of you . . . God sent me ahead of you to preserve for you a remnant on earth and to save your lives by a great deliverance."[11]

Joseph later added these words of reassurance: "You intended to harm me, but God intended it for good to accomplish what is now being done, the saving of many lives."[12]

Do you know that no matter how Satan, others, or this fallen world harm you, God can repurpose it for good to accomplish bigger plans than you could imagine? For all who believe, we will someday see that God not only repurposes our pain, turning it for good, but also that He used our surrendered difficulty to save the lives of others.

The hope of redemption is our certainty that, impossible as it seems today, the evil and pain in our lives *will* get repurposed for good as we continue trusting God with our lives.

When reunited with his brothers and dad, Joseph saw the glorious end of God's good plan.

And Joseph smiled through the tears.

Someday, believer, you will be reunited with loved ones too. You will see your Redeemer face-to-face. All around you, in senses beyond your earthly five senses, in ways you cannot imagine, you will see how God worked the evil and pain in your life for good. You will weep tears of joy.

And you will smile through the tears.

# CHAPTER 12

# Rescue from Above

---

We must meet the uncertainties of this world
with the certainty of the world to come.
*A. W. Tozer,* Of God and Men

*When my wife gave birth* to our son, she, like generations of women before her, had no epidural or pain medications. I did my best to cheer her along. But really, I was trying to keep *myself* together. I was witnessing human agony unlike any I'd ever seen.

Having watched the excruciating pain of childbirth, it amazes me that any woman has more than one child. And yet many do. Hundreds of millions do. Why would a smart, experienced person knowingly choose to go through that pain *again*? Why do so many desire, even ache, to experience one of the worst sufferings known to humanity . . . *again*?

Second-, third-, and fourth-time mothers willingly invite that pain because they know it is temporary. They also believe that the resulting joy and fulfillment of giving birth to a child will be lifelong. So enduring will that joy be that, even with its ups and downs, the lasting joy of motherhood overshadows the temporary suffering of childbirth.

It is hope that carries a mother through such pain. Hope that momentary, excruciating suffering will lead to lasting, exhilarating love. In a similar way, God promises believers that the worst pain we endure in this life is temporary. That it will someday be overshadowed by the massively longer and larger enduring good we will experience in His presence.

As a mother in labor fixes her mind on the arrival of her child, so we fix our minds on our future deliverance, the coming moment when our temporary pain will transition into unending joy.

This is the hope of deliverance. For the Christian, our ultimate deliverance will be the moment when Christ returns. We hope in this coming rescue.

Paul thrived in his prison of pain by lifting his thoughts outside his prison walls to this hope of rescue. He wrote, "I consider that our present sufferings are not worth comparing with the glory that will be revealed in us."[1]

Along with us, Paul declares that planet Earth is groaning for the rescue that will be ours when Christ returns: "The creation waits in eager expectation . . . in hope that the creation itself will be liberated from its bondage to decay and brought into the freedom and glory of the children of God."[2]

When Christ returns, He will re-create the earth to be new again, unpolluted by evil. He will restore us as well into bodies that have no sickness, no sin bent, no need for pain sensors.

Paul likens our lifelong struggle on earth to the grueling pangs of childbirth:

> We know that the whole creation has been groaning as in the pains of childbirth right up to the present time. Not only so, but we ourselves, who have the firstfruits of the Spirit, groan inwardly as we wait eagerly for our adoption to sonship, the redemption of our bodies.[3]

## Rescue from Above

> We were under great pressure, far
> beyond our ability to endure, so that we
> despaired of life itself. Indeed, we felt we
> had received the sentence of death.
> *2 Corinthians 1:8-9*

Louie Zamperini was an American track star and Olympian when World War II erupted.[4] He enlisted in the U.S. Army Air Corps and was assigned to a B-24 Liberator bomber. When that plane crashed in the Pacific Ocean, Louie survived on the open water for forty-seven days, fighting off sharks as well as starvation, sunburn, and dehydration. The Japanese then captured Louie, and so began his struggle to survive abuse, torture, and malnutrition in prison camps.

Louie endured unthinkable suffering for three years.

To me, the most fascinating moment in Louie's story is a brief six-day period. In August 1945, Japan surrendered to the United States—after the U.S. dropped atomic bombs on Hiroshima and Nagasaki.

World War II was over. And yet, in prison camps across Japan, sadistic Japanese prison guards continued to beat and torture American prisoners of war—like Louie. These prison guards knew the war was over. They knew they had been defeated. But they weren't about to let their suffering prisoners know. Louie continued to face beatings from a Japanese prison guard who knew Japan had lost the war.

Louie was a victor, but he was still living in an emaciated, diseased body and in an enemy prison camp. It took a number of days for some Japanese prison guards to admit defeat and abandon their posts.

In the spiritual history of humanity, we Christians find ourselves in precisely the same moment. When Christ died on the cross and rose from the dead, our spiritual enemy was defeated. Satan came into this world "to steal and kill and destroy."[5] In the moment of Christ's resurrection, every supernatural being in the universe knew that heaven had won the war. Evil *is* defeated.

The bloody cross and the empty tomb forever changed the struggle between good and evil. Like Louie in the Japanese prison camp, we now find ourselves in a brief moment after the enemy's defeat, but *before* our final deliverance. Satan has been defeated, but he has not yet been *sentenced* and brought to justice.

In this world, we wait—wounded by our pain and suffering—for God's rescue to be final and complete. Scripture calls us believers "conquerors" and "victors." And yet, in our hurting, we surely don't feel like conquering victors.

Presently, we live in enemy territory, in broken bodies.

Satan, who brought death, suffering and disease into our world, knows he is crushed. But like those guards at the Japanese prison camps, Satan continues to thrash about, inflicting pain until he can no longer get away with it—the day Christ returns to throw him into the lake of fire.[6]

This is the dark underbelly of Scripture's "already/not yet" tension. Our enemy is *already* defeated, but *not yet* sentenced to the lake of fire, where he will soon be confined to suffer so that justice will be served. He remains on the loose.

Jesus predicted this period of tension, in which we find ourselves. He warned His followers that it would be difficult to have faith during this chapter of the story: "Before long, the world will not see me anymore . . ."[7] He explained that, after defeating death and evil on the cross, He would go "to prepare a place for you[.] And if I go and prepare a place for you, I will come back and take you to be with me that you also may be where I am."[8]

For a season, we who follow Christ are freed victors—but we're still living in enemy territory. Jesus continued:

> "Peace I leave with you; my peace I give you. I do not give to you as the world gives. Do not let your hearts be troubled and do not be afraid.
>
> "You heard me say, 'I am going away and I am coming back to you.' . . . *I have told you now before it happens, so that when it does happen you will believe. I will not say much more to you, for the prince of this world [Satan] is coming.*"[9]

Until studying for this chapter, I had not noticed what Jesus says here: "The prince of this world [Satan] is coming." You don't hear Easter sermons about it. When Jesus gives His parting words to the disciples, he warns them that Satan will prowl planet Earth until Jesus returns to judge the world. Because of that, Jesus also warns of persecution and difficulty as we believers await His return.[10]

For six days, Louie and the other American prisoners lived as freed victors, but they were still enduring in enemy territory in malnourished bodies with an enemy who lied, claiming the war had not ended. And this is also where we find ourselves.

Until Christ returns, Satan is making a final furious push to destroy and torture humanity under his sadistic control. The apostle John refers to this in the book of Revelation: "He is filled with fury, because he knows that his time is short."[11] We know several things about our defeated enemy,[12] who, until his judgment, thrashes about like a snagged fish, hook in mouth:

- He is "now at work" as "the prince of the power of the air" or "the commander of the powers in the unseen world."[13]

- He blinds the minds of unbelievers and enslaves them in evil.[14]

- He is currently the ruler of this world until Christ returns to cast him out.[15]
- He uses unbelievers as slave laborers in his war machine to persecute God's people.[16]
- He works in the unseen forces, influencing the thoughts of unbelievers and influencing world politics, ideas, opinions, and cultures.[17]
- He still prowls about like a roaring lion, looking for souls to devour.[18]

All of earth, as it were, is his prison camp, full of forced slave laborers. This is why Christ came to set the captives free.[19]

We who trust in Christ are free from the power of the deceiver. But if we don't claim our freedom, the enemy is happy to have us living like he is still in charge—even though he isn't.

And so we live each day knowing we have "already" been freed from our enemy—but also knowing we are "not yet" home. As Louie and the malnourished prisoners fixed their eyes on the sky, looking for American warplanes to come free them, so we also fix our eyes on the clouds.[20] We live in the daily hope of our soon-to-be-completed rescue when Christ will return to take us out of these prison ruins, out of these broken bodies, and into heaven.

Our story is not yet done. Our rescue, which has begun, is not yet completed. Christ has defeated evil. He shared in our humanity "so that by his death he might break the power of him who holds the power of death—that is, the devil—and free those who all their lives were held in slavery by their fear of death."[21]

But Scripture emphasizes for our lifetimes this truth: "Yet at present we do not see everything subject" to Christ.[22]

Louie and other suffering prisoners encouraged each other to persevere, to endure, to keep waiting for the day when they would be freed entirely. In the same way, we believers cheer each other along to persevere during our wait: "Let us hold unswervingly to the hope we profess, for he who promised is faithful."[23]

———

While Louie's suffering seemed endless, it was only the *illusion* of endless suffering. After three years of suffering, Louie returned to America to live a thriving life in California for more than seventy years, well into his nineties.

Even as it felt and looked as though his suffering would never end, Louie's freedom had *already* been won. We often feel the same way. Paul felt this way too. He writes in Scripture that he didn't know how much longer he could make it through his suffering: "We were under great pressure, far beyond our ability to endure, so that we despaired of life itself. Indeed, we felt we had received the sentence of death."[24]

But Paul survived by reminding himself that Christ has defeated evil and will continue sustaining us until the moment He removes us out of this war zone: "He has delivered us from such a deadly peril, and he will deliver us again. On him we have set our hope that he will continue to deliver us."[25]

Paul fixed his hope on a rescue that is past, present, and future.

- **Past:** Christ already "has delivered us from" evil. Your victory over pain and evil *has already been accomplished* through Christ's death and resurrection.
- **Present:** While we live as victors in enemy territory, "we have set our hope . . ." on this: *"He will continue to deliver us."*
- **Future:** God "will continue to deliver us." *God is not going to abandon us now.*

Like Paul, we continue fixing our eyes on and arranging our lives around the "hope that he will continue to deliver us."

British writer G. K. Chesterton put it this way: "As long as matters are really hopeful, hope is a mere flattery or platitude; it is only when everything is hopeless that hope begins to be a strength at all . . . Hope means hoping when things are hopeless, or it is no virtue at all."[26]

Paul agreed: "We ourselves . . . wait eagerly for . . . the redemption of our bodies. For in this hope we were saved. But hope that is seen is no hope at all. Who hopes for what they already have? But if we hope for what we do not yet have, we wait for it patiently."[27]

And again Scripture encourages us: "Against all hope, Abraham in hope believed and so became the father of many nations."[28]

In each of our thorns, pains, and difficulties, we make a decision. You and I decide for ourselves if we will choose this kind of hope. And in that choice, we become one of two kinds of people:

- *negative people* with no hope for the future, constantly weighed down and defined by past and present suffering
- or, like Paul, we "set our hope" on the rescue already begun and soon to be finished; we become *joy-filled, peace-filled people*, even in our temporary prisons and difficulties.

God cheers us along, encouraging us to make the hope choice:

- "*Be joyful in hope*, patient in affliction, faithful in prayer."[29]
- And "May the God of *hope* fill you with all joy and peace as you trust in him, so that you may *overflow with hope* by the power of the Holy Spirit."[30]
- Because "[God] has delivered . . . and he will deliver us again. *On him we have set our hope* that he will continue to deliver us."[31]
- And "the eyes of the LORD are on those who fear him, on those whose *hope is in his unfailing love*."[32]

For thousands of years, God's people have been looking to the horizon and fixing their hope on rescue from above. The psalmist prayed, "My soul faints with longing for your salvation, but *I have put my hope in your word.*"[33]

And Scripture declares this:

> For the grace of God has appeared that offers salvation to all people. It teaches us to say "No" to ungodliness and worldly passions . . . in this present age, *while we wait for the blessed hope—the appearing of the glory of our great God and Savior, Jesus Christ,* who gave himself for us to redeem us from all wickedness."[34]

> Our citizenship is in heaven. And we eagerly await a Savior from there, the Lord Jesus Christ.
> *Philippians 3:20*

One day in the prison camp, Louie heard the roar of massive American aircraft engines. American prisoners of war looked heavenward to see the sun glinting off the polished aluminum hulls of massive B-29 Superfortress bombers.

Soon swarms of American fighter planes darkened the sky in a show of force. Some dropped packages, food, and news magazines that described how the war had ended days earlier.

And in that moment, the tables turned in the prison camps. The Japanese guards, so brazen and bold in the past, fled for the surrounding forests. Prisoners stood tall with authority. They overtook the guards' offices. They torched fences with fire and feasted on food dropped from above.

In a similar way, believers in Christ today can claim that Satan and his forces no longer have authority to deceive and intimidate Christ's people. Demons withdraw when we worship in full-hearted belief that Jesus has actually won the war, when we live with full-hearted belief that our enemy is defeated and will soon be judged.

Of the moment when the American prisoners realized their side had won, Laura Hillenbrand, author of *Unbroken*, writes, "In the midst of the running, celebrating men, Louie stood on wavering legs, emaciated, sick, and dripping wet. In his tired mind, two words were repeating themselves over and over: *"I'm free! I'm free! I'm free!"*[35]

No matter how emaciated, sick, or wavering we find ourselves to be in the prisons of our earthly pain, we too can proclaim, because of the cross, "I'm free! I'm free! I'm free!"

As prisoners in skeletal bodies awaited their full deliverance out of the labor camps, American planes continually dropped food provisions from above. And the prisoners, with stomachs that had starved for years, began gorging themselves. Some sang. Some shouted. Some danced in conga lines.

Hillenbrand tells of one prisoner, J. O. Young, who wrote this in his diary: "As four years prisoners . . . there's no such thing as being satisfied after eating. You either don't have enough, or as we are all now so darn full you're in misery. There's just one thing left to say as we bunk down for the night . . . that it's wonderful to be Americans and free men. And it's a might [*sic*] hard job even now to realize we're free men."[36]

Indeed, we who trust in Christ can equally celebrate our victory. We feast daily on rations that God drops down from above (see part 2, "Feeding on Heaven's Strength"). When we gather to worship with other believers, we sing of our freedom (some even dance in conga lines!). And yet in the struggles of this broken, prison shambles of a world, "it's a might [*sic*] hard job even now to realize we're free."

Louie and the others would wait almost another week before getting physically delivered out of the wreckage of the Japanese prison camps. Even after the guards fled (and Satan flees you when you submit to God's plan in your life, see James 4:7), the men still lived among the shambles of the prison. They still lived in the shambles of malnourished and beaten bodies. But they were freed from their captors, and food fell from above.

In the same way, our enemy is defeated. History and humanity wait for Christ and His forces to descend from above and fully enforce that victory, with all its freedom.

We are free in heart but remain tattered in our bodies. We are victors, awaiting our enemy captor's arrest, trial, and imprisonment. Through our sore rib cages, with tear-filled eyes, some days we doubt if such a victory can really be ours. We naturally wonder, some days, if we will ever see our Savior bursting through the clouds. But we fix our eyes on that hope. We arrange our lives around it. We cling to it by faith. We live knowing that unlimited food, strength, and care await us, as do loving family members who have gone before.

And yet, as we know and claim this, we wait in our worn-out bodies for a final transport, for the day of final justice, for the time when we see with our eyes what we already believe with our hearts—the full restoration of our persons. The full judgment of our enemy. The full joy of a new land, a restored land. All these and so much more await the soul who trusts in Christ.

Isaiah the prophet set his hope on this day:

> And the glory of the LORD will be revealed,
>    and all people will see it together.
>        For the mouth of the LORD has
>        spoken . . .
>
> See, the Sovereign LORD comes with power,
>    and he rules with a mighty arm.
> See, his reward is with him,
>    and his recompense accompanies him.[37]

Jesus put it this way: "I say to all of you: From now on you will see the Son of Man sitting at the right hand of the Mighty One and coming on the clouds of heaven."[38]

In that day Jesus, who is the one true God, will not appear as a sacrificial lamb or suffering servant, but as King of kings and Lord of lords. With an army of angels, a sword of truth, and eyes of fire, He will justly judge the evil one and the evils of history.

Early believers in Christ "turned to God from idols to serve the living and true God, and to wait for his Son from heaven, whom he raised from the dead—Jesus, who rescues us from the coming wrath."[39]

John the disciple, writing from his literal prison, fixed his eyes on the same hope: "Look, he is coming with the clouds, and every eye will see him, even those who pierced him . . . will mourn because of him. So shall it be! Amen."[40]

Christ's return will cause mourning for His violent enemies. But for us who trust in Him, our souls will collapse into tears of joy. Conga lines of eternal celebration when we hear our Mighty Savior declare from the clouds, "I Am the Alpha and the Omega . . . who is, and who was, and who is to come, the Almighty."[41]

Until then, He promises this to all who grow tired, confused, and doubtful as they await His arrival:

> He gives strength to the weary
> and increases the power of the weak.
> Even youths grow tired and weary
> and young men stumble and fall;
> but those who hope in the LORD
> will renew their strength.
> They will soar on wings like eagles;
> they will run and not grow weary . . .[42]

"Run and not grow weary." Those would have been encouraging words to Louie Zamperini, the Olympian runner, as he awaited his rescue from above.

Let those words encourage you as you await your rescue. Yes, you will be sustained here in these shambles of a labor camp. Even more, fix your hope on this: You will be rescued from above.

———

Our great hope of rescue is not only that we will be delivered *out of* the pains of this world; it is equally a hope that we will be delivered *into* the joys of a new world, the truest land of the free. Revelation 21 describes it:

> Then I saw a new heaven and a new earth . . . prepared as a bride beautifully dressed for her husband. And I heard a loud voice from the throne saying, "Look! God's dwelling place is now among the people, and he will dwell with them. They will be his people, and God himself will be with them and be their God. *He will wipe every tear from their eyes. There will be no more death or mourning or crying or pain, for the old order of things has passed away.*"[43]

Joni Eareckson Tada, who lives daily with the "thorn" of a wheelchair, broken spine, and paralysis, puts the hope of rescue this way:

> "I haven't been cheated out of being a complete person—I'm just going through a forty- or fifty-year delay, and God stays with me even through that.
>
> I now know the meaning of being "glorified." It's the time, after my death here, when I'll be on my feet dancing."[44]

We live daily with hope of passage into a world no less alive or gratifying than the present, but infinitely more colorful, fruitful, warm, positively emotional, and problem free. Thorn-free, anxiety-free, pain-free in ways we cannot imagine. We have, as of yet, never known anything like it.

The prophet Isaiah describes it:

> The desert and the parched land will be glad;
>     the wilderness will rejoice and blossom.
> Like the crocus, it will burst into bloom;
>     it will rejoice greatly and shout for joy . . .
> they will see the glory of the LORD,
>     the splendor of our God.
> Strengthen the feeble hands,
>     steady the knees that give way;
> say to those with fearful hearts,
>     "Be strong, do not fear;
> your God will come,
>     he will come with vengeance;
> with divine retribution
>     he will come to save you."[45]

C. S. Lewis, in his essay "The Weight of Glory," summarizes:

It is promised, firstly, that we shall be with Christ; secondly, that we shall be like Him; thirdly, with an enormous wealth of imagery, that we shall have "glory"; fourthly, that we shall, in some sense, be fed, feasting, or entertained; and finally, that we shall have some sort of official position in the universe— ruling cities, judging angels, being pillars of God's temple.[46]

We cannot fully know what heaven is like, but we see crude glimpses in the contrast between Louie as a malnourished prisoner of war and then as a postwar American in a land of abundance, freedom, and plenty.

Heaven will be a place where we are delighted in and patted on the back, with the approval that all children long for (and most grownups long for too). This approval, this glory, will be ours, given freely to nations of people from every century and continent who have hoped in Christ.

> The promise of glory is the promise almost incredible and only possible by the work of Christ, that some of us, that any of us who really chooses, shall actually survive . . . shall find approval, shall please God . . . to be a real ingredient in the divine happiness . . . to be loved by God, not merely pitied, but delighted in as an artist delights in his work or a father in a son—it seems impossible—a weight or burden of glory which our thoughts can hardly sustain. But so it is.[47]

After describing this future glory, C. S. Lewis returned (like the apostle Paul) to our present reality. The shambles of the prison camp in which we presently find ourselves feeding on God's promises and from which we continually look to the clouds for our final deliverance.

> Meanwhile, the cross comes before the crown and tomorrow is a Monday morning. A cleft has opened in the pitiless walls of the world, and we are invited to follow our great Captain inside. The following Him is, of course, the essential point.[48]

Jesus spoke of the difficulty we endure as we await His return to take us into this better future:

> "You will grieve, but your grief will turn to joy. A woman giving birth to a child has pain because her time has come; but when her baby is born she forgets the anguish because of her joy that a child is born into the world. So with you: Now is your time of grief, but I will see you again and you will rejoice, and no one will take away your joy."[49]

Postscript: In moments of joy, my wife weeps tears of joy with a freedom and abandon that I envy. Never have I seen her shed more tears of overwhelming joy than in those moments following the agony of childbirth.

After all those excruciating pains of labor, constantly driven forward by hope. Moved and moving through unthinkable pain, driven forward by the hope of future life. In that moment when the doctor cradles new, squirming life and then sets the child on my wife's chest, tears of joy overcome her. And it is beautiful. A fullness of emotion so powerful that some of us fear it. But it is good. And wonderful.

That overwhelming joy is a glimpse, a small picture, of the joy that will be ours when Christ bursts through the clouds. When all of our waiting and hoping, believing and faith-ing, delivers.

When the birth pains of this world are forever over and we are forever delivered. Forever rescued. Forever in a place of no pain, no suffering—and not only empty of those, but entirely filled with the good of God, with oceans of pleasure, joy, and goodness that we only ever felt droplets of on fallen earth.

> Dear friends, now we are children of God,
> and what we will be has not yet been made
> known. But we know that when Christ
> appears, we shall be like him, for we shall
> see him as he is. All who have this hope in
> him purify themselves, just as he is pure.
>
> *1 John 3:2-3*

# CHAPTER 13

# Traveling Songs

One comes to realize, what one always
admitted theoretically, that there is nothing
here that will do us good: the sooner we
are safely out of this world the better.

C. S. Lewis, Yours, Jack

*These great hopes we're learning*—that God is going to rescue us, that God will redeem our pain for good, that the shores of heaven are waiting—some days, these hopes seem as near as the breath in our nostrils. Other days, if you're like me, these hopes feel impossibly distant.

Some days, we find ourselves too exhausted to grasp for the hopes of heaven. They can seem irrelevant in our prisons of pain and fatigue.

I have been doing my best to carve out sturdy handles of hope you can grab on to. But no matter how solid these handles are, some days, we will not have the strength to reach for them.

It reminds me of a TV show called *Wipeout*. It's an action game show in which unfortunate contestants attempt to jump their way through an obstacle course of unbearable feats. The show's creators intentionally design impossible physical challenges, which produce fantastic wipeouts from contestants who splash into water, mud, or goop.

Picture a contestant attempting to stabilize himself on a gigantic spinning wheel. There, a few feet away, is a handle that he can jump toward. So he jumps. But little does he know that the handle is wet or greased with something. He weighs too much. His hand slips. And he wipes out, falling into the mud.

I realize that, even if I could give you perfect handles of hope to grab, some days, life will feel like you're a contestant on *Wipeout*. Your trouble weighs too much. Your hands slip. You crash.

Only, nobody laughs when we fall. And there's no warm towel waiting off-camera.

When hoping is hardest, that's when it matters most.

So I want to give you not one or two handles of hope to reach for in your storm, in your spinning wheel of a life; I want to give you four. If your grip on one slips, you can grab on to another. And if, like me, you fall, then you have four handles with which to lift yourself back up.

Here are four handles of hope you can grab on to by faith when things feel hopeless:

1. *The hope of rescue.* We set our minds on the hope that we will be delivered out of our pain. *No matter how bad it ever gets here, this is temporary. Life with Christ will be eternal* (see chapter 12, "Rescue from Above").

2. *The hope of redemption.* We remind ourselves that God is powerful enough to repurpose the evil and hurt in our lives for good. *The more painful it is now, the more beautiful it will be when we see God miraculously turn the pain for good* (see chapter 11, "Smiling through Tears").

3. *The hope of reaching heaven.* When we seem trapped in the sun-cooked desert of this world, we remind ourselves that these dunes will give way to the life-giving fresh waters of heaven. And in our weaknesses today, *where our limits dead-end, God's limitless begins* (see chapter 10, "Trading Limits for Limitless").

4. In this chapter, we are learning that while we await rescue, redemption, and heaven, we have another hope—*the hope of*

*refuge.* Our comfort is this: *God is with us and will sustain us through the most difficult moments of our lives and eternities.*

For thousands of years, believers have clung to these hopes by reciting, thinking, or even singing them. When we declare these hopes to ourselves or to others, we join an ancient rite—the singing of "Traveling Songs."

Traveling Songs are not always sung as songs. Sometimes they are walked, sighed, or just believed. They are reminders of where home is, why we're headed there, how temporary our hurts are, and who is with us on the journey.

A traveling song is the sort of thing you can take with you anywhere. You can take it into an operating room—when you're stripped of your clothes, your phone, your glasses. Even your wedding ring and piercings have to stay behind when they wheel you into surgery. But not your Traveling Songs. They go with you. Because you carry them in your soul.

Oppressors may steal your home, your money, even your identity. But they can never steal your songs. Not the ones you carry in your blood. The strongest Christians, the sturdiest believers, are simply people who have learned to carry Traveling Songs (their words vary, but their unchanging themes do not) in their bones.

Multitudes of believers who predate us have clung to these well-worn, time-proven hopes. They've held firmly with vice-like faith. They've held on through earthquakes, famines, and persecutions. They've held with a grip that carried them over the threshold of death, that moment when the faith they held so tightly lifted them up out this broken life and into heaven.

Generations of spiritual ancestors spread beneath us like the roots of an ancient, massive tree. Their lives verify our hope in

Christ. They sang Traveling Songs long before us. They proved the sturdy trustworthiness of a life built around these themes.

We are young leaves on this massive tree of faith. It has been growing on every continent, across thousands of languages and cultures for millennia. When we wonder if these hopes are worth building a life around, we need only look back, look down, at the hundreds of millions who have gone before us. Never once has a sincere believer in the hopes of Christ been abandoned in her hope, in his hope.

In this sprawling root system of Christianity, stretching into the firmaments of human history, we find a galaxy of Traveling Songs. Songs of hope. Of future. Of assurance. Songs that thundered confidence into warriors. Songs that whispered comfort to the wounded. They've been written in thousands of languages. Sung on every continent. Groaned upon deathbeds. Hundreds more Traveling Songs will be written today, sung in rice patties, in palaces, in boardrooms, and in bathrooms.

The themes of the great Traveling Songs remain unchanged through cultures and centuries:

- This is not the end for Christ's people.
- It only gets better from here because of Christ.
- Even the worst evil will be turned for good by Christ.
- Our suffering is temporary, and our glory will be eternal, in Christ.
- Our God will sustain us through the worst of it, just as He sustained Christ on earth.

God's travelers sing, shout, whisper, and believe these themes as we journey through a jagged world.

Our ancestors sang Traveling Songs in handwritten pages. Some declared them from pulpits. Millions have sung them from literal prisons, others from slave labor camps. The martyrs sang these themes on guillotines. Historians document Christians who sang them even as they watched their own bodies catch ablaze, lighting from the feet up, in Nero's gardens. Today, at this very moment, Christians in parts of the Arab world, China, and North Korea sing them through torture, starvation, and execution.

An Israelite worship leader wrote one of the early Traveling Songs, part of our Scriptures today. It goes like this:

> God is our refuge and strength,
>   *an ever-present help in trouble.*
> Therefore we will not fear, though the
>   earth give way
>     and the mountains fall into
>       the heart of the sea,
> though its waters roar and foam
>   and the mountains quake
>     with their surging.[1]

The Bible records 150 of these early Hebrew Traveling Songs in the book of Psalms.

This traveling song and thousands of others like it are songs of refuge. They shout the reality that even *in* our pain, even *in* our waiting, God is with us to help us. Like a good parent or a loving friend, He is with us to help us, feel for us, and walk with us through the trouble.

When I speak a song of refuge, I expel the doubt from my soul, reminding me that not only does God deliver me out of my pain, but He is also present with me *in* my pain. He is ever-present with you to sustain you, uphold you, and preserve you *in* your trouble. He will not abandon you in your crescendo of pain when you most need Him.

He is present with you in the waiting room. Present with you in the hospital bed. Present with you at the funeral home. Present with you when you're alone in your car, feeling like the whole world is against you.

The hope of refuge is the hope that when God does not immediately still the storm, end the battle, or heal the sickness, He will sustain and strengthen you until the very-soon time when He *does* still the storm, end the battle, or heal the sickness.

- "In your distress," He hears.
- "In your storm," He cares.
- "In your difficulty," He sustains.
- "In the worst of the worst," He is present with you to uphold you as you endure a pain that will, when you look back on it all, seem impossibly brief. (And yet, like a loving parent, holding a child's hand in a hospital room, He knows how severely you hurt in this moment.)

Eugene Peterson opened my eyes to see the sturdy beauty of Traveling Songs in his book *A Long Obedience in the Same Direction*, which studies Psalms 121 to 126. Explaining this theme of God's presence with us, Peterson writes these words:

> All suffering, all pain, all emptiness, all disappointment is seed: sow it in God and he will, finally, bring a crop of joy from it.
>
> It is clear in Psalm 126 that the one who wrote it and those who sang it were no strangers to the dark side of things. They carried the painful memory of exile in their bones and the scars of oppression on their backs. They knew the deserts of the heart and the nights of weeping. They knew what it meant to sow in tears.[2]

Peterson writes that many people, even well-meaning believers, never get to the place where they really live like this world is not home. We resist learning the Traveling Songs because we resist operating from the assumption that we are just visiting this world. He put it this way:

> A person has to be thoroughly disgusted with the way things are to find the motivation to set out on the Christian way. As long as we think the next election might eliminate crime and establish justice or another scientific breakthrough might save the environment or another pay raise might push us over the edge of anxiety into a life of tranquillity, we are not likely to risk the arduous uncertainties of the life of faith. A person has to get fed up with the ways of the world before he, before she, acquires an appetite for the world of grace."[3]

Peterson writes about "the turning point marking the transition from a dreamy nostalgia for a better life [here and now] to a rugged pilgrimage of discipleship in faith, from complaining about how bad things are to pursuing all things good."[4]

Referencing that great root system of ancestors, from which our faith grows, Peterson writes, "A Christian who has David in his bones, Jeremiah in his bloodstream, Paul in his fingertips, and Christ in his heart will know how much and how little value to put on his own momentary feelings and the experience of the past week."[5]

Deep in that rich complex of ancestors we find God's beloved people, Israel, who learned thousands of years ago to see themselves as travelers in a foreign land: "Israel . . . became a pilgrim people, picking a path of peace and righteousness through the battlefields of falsehood and violence, finding a path to God through the labyrinth of sin."[6]

The peace that the Israelites enjoyed in their good God was

not a peace that depended on perfect circumstances or easy living. It was a peace that thrived *in* suffering.

> And *shalvah*, "prosperity." It has nothing to do with insurance policies or large bank accounts or stockpiles of weapons. The root meaning is leisure—the relaxed stance of one who knows that everything is all right because God is over us, with us, and for us in Jesus Christ. It is the security of being at home in a history that has a cross at its center. It is the leisure of the person who knows that every moment of our existence is at the disposal of God, lived under the mercy of God.[7]

The Israelites sang Traveling Songs on their arduous yearly pilgrimage to Jerusalem. Now we sing the same themes on our journey to a new City of Peace, the everlasting Promised Land.

How remarkable that these same themes, sung in Palestinian deserts some 3,500 years ago, were also sung by early African-American slaves, whose ancestors traveled through the Charleston, South Carolina, slave markets and into the antebellum South. A few generations later, they sang in their spirituals:

- "This world is not my home, I'm just a passing through."
- "Soon-a will be done with the troubles of this world."
- "Deep river, my home is over Jordan . . . Oh, don't you want to go, to that gospel feast, that Promised Land, where all is peace?"

Under the whip and injustice of slavery, which flies in the face of God's nature, these men and women of faith grabbed on to the hope of a better life, a future life with a good God in a good kingdom where there is no injustice, no whip, and no pain. A place where every wrong is made right.

John Newton was captain of an English slaving ship. He had spent his life trafficking African slaves. Then Newton trusted

Christ and cried out to be forgiven. As Newton learned the Bible, he realized the unspeakable cruelty, the evil he had thrust onto the souls he shipped from Africa. Newton then gave his life to end the trafficking of African slaves—a seemingly impossible cause that eventually succeeded in England and later spread to the United States.

Reflecting on God's outrageous forgiveness for his own crimes, Newton put his gratitude into words: "Amazing grace! how sweet the sound, that saved a wretch like me! I once was lost, but now am found, was blind, but now I see."

Newton's song may be the most recognized Christian hymn of our time, and it is a traveling song. It is a declaration of hope in Christ—that we are forgiven, that we have a future, that even our mistakes can be turned for good once we turn from them and cling to Christ.

Like so many Traveling Songs, "Amazing Grace" ends with a final stanza about heaven: "When we've been there ten thousand years, bright shining as the sun . . ."

History's greatest Traveling Songs lock our eyes and our hearts on heaven.

The eighth-century Irish hymn "Be Thou My Vision" builds to the final verse: "May I reach heaven's joys, O bright heaven's Sun."

"How Great Thou Art" closes with these words: "When Christ shall come with shout of acclamation and take me home, what joy shall fill my heart!"

Another traveling song crescendos: "Be still my soul! the hour is hastening on when we shall be forever with the Lord, when disappointment, grief, and fear are gone, sorrow forgot, love's purest joys restored."

"It Is Well with My Soul" anchors the soul in this hope: "O Lord, haste the day when my faith shall be sight, the clouds be rolled back as a scroll, the trump shall resound, and the Lord shall descend."

Still another, "On Christ the Solid Rock I Stand," ends, "When He shall come with trumpet sound, O may I then in Him be found; dressed in his righteousness alone, faultless to stand before the throne."

In every century, year, day, and hour of history, God's people have sung the shared, unchanging themes of our Traveling Songs, reminding each other and reminding ourselves that we will be delivered out of this world. Reminding ourselves and our spiritual siblings that *we will be sustained and strengthened until our deliverance.*

Our souls need Traveling Songs as much as John Newton's did, as much as those of our siblings who toiled under slavery in the antebellum South or in Rome. As much as the souls of our suffering brothers and sisters who are beaten, starved, and stripped in other regions of the world today.

Learning to live as strangers who are "just a passing through" means learning to be honest about our groans and aches in this world. And in that honesty, seeing our present pains as stepping-stones, on which we can leap our thoughts from this temporary world to the next, eternal one.

God's people have always found great joy in singing Traveling Songs. Joy in ancient Rome, as they sang before jeering, bloodthirsty crowds. Joy in the hearts of those arrested and thrust before the lions in the coliseums. Joy in the tobacco fields. Joy in the Soviet gulags. And surely—if we will recover the mind-set, the life song of a traveler—joy in our struggles and tribulations today.

It is right to long for the better land that is our home. But it is not a suicidal longing, not a despair at the difficulties of today's journey. We sing our Traveling Songs knowing that the same God who is mighty to save us is also faithful to *sustain* us.

He is with us in our trouble.

He is our refuge.

He is at this moment our hiding place.

He is listening, holding, caring.

And He is in the process of working His good and His purposes through us and for us.

He never once abandoned any single believer in the thick layers of travelers before us (grown like so many rings in the trunk of an ancient tree). He never once abandoned a single one before you, and He will never once abandon *you*.

Eugene Peterson explains the joy with which we can live our Traveling Songs: "Christian joy is not an escape from sorrow. Pain and hardship still come, but they are unable to drive out the happiness of the redeemed."[8]

When we grasp the temporary nature of our sufferings, the sure coming of our King, the future turning of all evil to good, the present help God is today *in* our troubles, then our journey home becomes a joyful one.

We call out to God in our difficulty, and, in superhuman ways, heaven's joy injects strength into our wobbling legs, our weary hearts. The journey through this barren land becomes one of sunrises, of campfires in the dark, of warm companionship and laughter, all received and daily delighted in as the strength that heaven sends to sustain its people on their journey home.

Impossibly long journeys become short trips when you have the right company. In Christ and in our millions of fellow travelers, both brothers and sisters, we have the company needed to sustain us on our journey home.

John Bunyan wrote one of the bestselling books of history, a literary classic. He wrote it from his own prison of pain, a literal jail cell. *The Pilgrim's Progress* declares the themes of Traveling Songs in story form. The main character, named Christian, is weighed down with shame, guilt, and questions. When he repents and believes in Christ, those weights get lifted. And yet he still has a long journey full of swamps, attacks, deceptions, temptations, cold, hunger, and vicious enemies on his journey to the "heavenly city."

Bunyan's literary classic has put steel into the backbones of countless Christians, teaching us to live as the travelers we actually are. We learn to long, like Bunyan, for "a place that can never be destroyed, one that is pure, and that fadeth not away, and it is laid up in heaven, and safe there, to be given, at the time appointed, to them that seek it with all their heart."[9]

Some of my favorite Traveling Songs were written around 1100 BC by King David. He commonly opens his songs with honest moans about the difficulties in his life. Sometimes David expresses his anger with God. He's honest about the doubts he feels. And slowly, line by line, verse by verse, David works his way toward the unchanging themes of God's goodness, God's ability to win in the end, God's future for those who trust in Him.

David does not betray God in the dark, but neither does he pretend all is light when the clouds of despair, attack, and death settle on his life.

In the same way today, our Traveling Songs can include honest moans about our feelings, doubts, and pains. As we drag those cares to God, we slowly but consistently move our eyes toward heaven, toward hope, toward redemption.

One by one, we turn our stumbling blocks into stepping-stones, leaping our way toward God in a faith that fully acknowledges the stubbed toes, the despairs, and the pains of our journey home.

Here are a few Traveling Songs in which David reminds himself that God is present with him *in* his difficulty and trouble.

When I called, you answered me . . .

Though I walk *in the midst of trouble*,
    you preserve my life.[10]


Do not fret because of those who are evil
    or be envious of those who do wrong;
for like the grass they will soon wither . . .

Take delight in the LORD
    and he will give you the desires
        of your heart . . .

The salvation of the righteous comes from
    the LORD;
        he is their stronghold *in time of trouble*.
The LORD helps them and delivers them;
    he delivers them from the
        wicked and saves them,
        because they take refuge in him."[11]


The LORD is a refuge for the oppressed,
    *a stronghold in times of trouble*.[12]


Truly my soul finds rest in God;
    my salvation comes from him.
Truly he is my rock and my salvation;
    he is my fortress, I will never be shaken . . .

Yes, my soul, find rest in God;
    my hope comes from him . . .
*Trust in him at all times, you people;*
    *pour out your hearts to him,*
    *for God is our refuge*.[13]

David shepherded sheep before becoming king. During that time, he likely wrote the most famous traveling song of all, a traveling song recited on battlefields from the ancient Near East to modern-day Iraq, and in World Wars I and II.

> The LORD is my shepherd, I shall not want.
>> He makes me lie down in green pastures.
> He leads me beside still waters.
>> He restores my soul.
> He leads me in paths of righteousness
>> for his name's sake.

> *Even though I walk through the valley of the*
>> *shadow of death,*
>> *I will fear no evil,*
> *for you are with me;*
>> *your rod and your staff,*
>> *they comfort me.*[14]

Here's another:

> Listen to my prayer, O God,
>> do not ignore my plea;
>> hear me and answer me.
> My thoughts trouble me and I am distraught . . .

> My heart is in anguish within me;
>> the terrors of death have fallen on me.
> Fear and trembling have beset me . . .

> *As for me, I call to God,*
>> *and the LORD saves me.*
> *Evening, morning and noon*
>> *I cry out in distress,*
>> *and he hears my voice.*
> *He rescues me unharmed*
>> *from the battle waged against me,*
>> *even though many oppose me.*[15]

No painted religious pretentions here. David throws all of his weight into real, human emotions, using them as stepping-stones to lead his mind, his heart, his self, away from the quicksand of despair and toward the sure promises of God's character and love.

This is what Traveling Songs can do for us every day of our journey through Rocky Flats. Get some Traveling Songs into your heart, and they will inject bravery and courage into your life.

Because of his Traveling Songs, because of the truths David built his life around, he became a powerful man. Mighty in God and in God's strength.

Long before he ran toward the bloodstained ultimate fighting champion Goliath, young David had already soaked his soul in the sureties and confidence of heaven. David, even younger and humanly alone as a shepherd, stepped *toward* the lion, coiled like a spring, teeth bared. David grabbed its hair in hand because he knew God's presence. He knew it in the prayers he wrote and in the songs he spoke aloud.

And he is just one of the roots, just one of our millions of ancestors, who have believed and who found God faithful.

Daniel looked dictators in the eyes and didn't flinch. He closed his eyes, breathed easy, and fell asleep next to hungry lions because he knew God's presence as more real than the heat of a lion's breath.

Others faced gallows—hanging towers built for their necks alone.

Furnaces—stoked to melting, just for them.

Armies—stretching toward the horizon like ants with glinting armor.

Raging rivers and drought-dry deserts.

Impassable seas and impossible opponents.

Wilderness, starvation, rebellion, crucifixion, betrayal, failure, regret.

The call to leave everything and start over.

And in all of it, to generation after generation, God's presence.

So real and tangible, sung from one thousand million lips.

His presence—the steely backbone of believers in every age and culture.

His presence—the spinal structure and support, strengthening the saints through centuries, through millennia.

And still strengthening more than two billion of us today who name Christ as Lord.

Let us be a generation that declares His faithfulness to the next, for He has proven Himself to be an ever-present help in time of trouble. He will be an ever-present help ten generations from now, when we have long left this world.

And today He is our *ever-present* help in time of trouble.

An ever-present hope in adversity.

An ever-present refuge in storm and difficulty.

Let's sing that song.

Let's rub these themes into the fabric of our souls.

Let's declare them with our hands, our choices, our lives, our voices.

The day is coming when we will stand, intermixed with the Christians who bled in Roman coliseums, with our siblings who struggled as American slaves, with John Newton and John Bunyan, with King David, and with millions of others who today sing the Traveling Songs from prisons in North Korea and Nigeria.

Then, with glorified, perfect bodies and with brand-new, pitch-perfect voices (a relief for me and many others), we will sing God's goodness in a chorus that no goose-bump concert or euphoria of this world can compare with.

And so, even in our trials now, we can begin singing. Whether by words, by steps forward, or by chosen faith, we can begin singing the themes of the ancient Traveling Songs.

Knowing that we are not alone in our singing.
And *you* are not alone in your believing.
I'm singing and believing—with you.
And with Him.
He is present,
with you.

# PART 5

# CARRIED

*The Pen and Paper*

# CHAPTER 14

# In Your Gethsemane

"My soul is overwhelmed with
sorrow to the point of death."
*Jesus Christ, Matthew 26:38*

*The story of humanity* can be told in thorns. It starts with a world that knew no thorns, no thistles, and no pain. That's the world God created. Perfect.

Thorns and thistles never should have existed. They enter the story, not as God's original creation, but as mutant contamination. The work of sin's radioactive fallout in Rocky Flats (see chapter 7).

Literal thorns enter early—in Genesis 3:18. And then we begin finding them in every family tree. Dysfunction, divorce, murder, hatred. Such thorns have infected every corner of creation. The blood-drawing prick of a rosebush testifies that nothing is immune to the weed-like spread of evil on earth.

Minutes after humanity turned away from God, thorns and thistles sprouted as a first fallout of sin. So it's no accident that when Jesus came to free us from evil, He had literal thorns stabbed into His body.

Matthew, who was present at Jesus' crucifixion, tells us, "The governor's soldiers took Jesus . . . stripped him . . . and then twisted together a crown of thorns and set it on his head."[1]

Here is the perfect Creator who had handed humanity a thorn-free world. Here He has come to rescue us from the mess we have made of our planet and our lives. And humans, His created beings, twist together a crown of the thorns grown from our own consequences. We press it into the tender skin of His forehead.

What a picture of Father God's heart! Him sitting quietly, absorbing our evils, our pains, our flaws as they pressed into Him so He could overpower them for us.

The story doesn't end there. The story still has not ended. The day is coming when Jesus returns and takes His people to a "new heaven and a new earth."[2] And then, there will be no more thorns. Instead, we will eat from the youth-restoring, eternal-life-giving "tree of life" that graced the Garden of Eden before sin.[3] This tree, free of thorns, will have fruit with the opposite effect—"the healing of the nations."[4] In that day, the effects of sin and all of its contamination will be history.

Until then, we followers of Christ travel by faith through a world still infected with thorns. And in this journey, we will each find thorns staked into the tender flesh of our lives.

Here's one difference between your thorn in the flesh and God's thorn in the flesh: Jesus could have chosen at any time to remove His thorn. But He didn't.

When we wonder why God allows our temporary thorns in the flesh, we can remind ourselves that He also allowed His own, much worse thorn in the flesh. He will never ask you to suffer any more than He Himself suffered on his mission to redeem humanity.

Why did God allow His own thorn in the flesh?

- He allowed it so He can relate to you in your pain (see Hebrews 4:15).

- He also allowed it because it was *through* His carrying of that thorn that He made a way for us to be delivered, once and for all, from our own thorns. Through His chosen weakness, we're made strong.

At the cross, Jesus' pain and suffering cut an opening into the fabric of the universe, an opening through which all of God's healing, forgiveness, and power invaded the darkness of humanity.

> Man of Sorrows, what a name
> for the Son of God who came.
> *Philip P. Bliss*

We began our journey with a note about the Greek word Paul chose to write when describing his own "thorn in the flesh." He did not use the word for a thistle on a rosebush or raspberry bush. Instead, Paul chose a word that in other ancient texts of that time meant "stake."

Other than tent stakes, we rarely use the word *stake* today. We usually use another word that means the same thing: *nail*.

In addition to the smaller "thorns" that pierced the skin of Jesus' forehead and scalp, He also had three large stakes driven through His flesh. Stakes impaling Jesus' flesh held the squirming heaviness of his body until His punctured lungs drowned in His own blood. Jesus simultaneously suffocated and bled to death.

Many religions worship distant, powerful, imagined gods who cannot relate to human pain and suffering. Gods who know nothing of the difficulty we humans carry around with us. Gods who know nothing of our thorns. Not so with Jesus. The pain He endured makes Him a Healer who sympathizes with our pain. He understands our pain.

He has felt your pain and feels your pain with you today.

When we worship Jesus for eternity, we will not worship a soft-handed prince, a trust-fund baby who never saw combat. We will worship a spiritually muscular Being who willingly lowered Himself, ventured into our hell, fought our demons, carried our death, ate our pains, drank our suffering. And if anyone ever doubts His claim to the throne of the universe, they will only need to look at His hands. Because while eternity will lack thorns, we will always have vivid evidence of their existence—in the gaping cavities of the King's hands and feet.

In Jesus, we find the one true God of the universe, entirely powerful and in the process of delivering us from our pain, but also entirely human and hurting together with us, longing *with us* for the redemption, repurposing, and healing of our pain.

It is one thing to know that Almighty God is with you on your journey through this fallen world. It is something else to also know that He Himself has walked through the jagged rubble of this planet *as a human*. The same rocks that injure us have cut His skin. These same thorns have drawn His blood. He knows the discouragement of the darkness all around you. He knows the full range of emotions you experience—highs, lows, flatlines, frustrations. He knows the limitations of a human body, the pains of human flesh.

Christ relates not only to our severe, life-defining pain but also to our daily struggles and temptations. His carpenter hands know the stab of a splinter under a fingernail. He knows the warmth of a salty tear on His cheek. He probably even knows what it's like to bite his tongue while eating. He knows what it feels like to have to go to the bathroom. He knows the feeling of a sneeze. He knows the emptiness of rejection, the frustration of being misunderstood, the inward bruising of slander.

He relates to our physical pain. And, just as much, He relates to our emotional pain.

> I get no further than Gethsemane: and am
> daily thankful that that scene, of all others
> in Our Lord's life, did not go unrecorded.
>
> *C. S. Lewis*

Let's walk together, quietly, into the hours *just before* Jesus met the thorns of His torture and suffering.

A few hours before the physical agony of the cross, we find Jesus in emotional agony. He has sneaked away to a favorite place of His, a garden outside Jerusalem's city walls. Inside the walls, thousands of torches pierce the darkness, a city teeming with tourists, all there to celebrate the festival of the year, Passover. (A holiday that, not incidentally, celebrates God's redemption through shedding the blood of a spotless, sacrificial lamb, reminding believers of their rescue out of slavery, out of a foreign land.)

Many of the tourists packing Jerusalem admire Jesus. Thousands are talking about Him, even now as they finish their ceremonial Passover dinners. They've heard of Jesus' miracles. Many have seen Jesus heal the blind or raise the dead to life. Thousands have eaten the fish He multiplied. Some even believe He is Messiah—God among us to save us. A whole mob of them spent the week chanting those exact words.

In this moment of personal emotional turmoil, Jesus could have chosen to remain among His admirers. He could have found human comfort in their backslaps, their desire to be near a celebrity leader, their talking all night long about His miracles. Instead, Jesus walks away from the warmth and comfort of other people. Out into the cool evening dark where He has always found His true comfort, with His heavenly Father.

He walks beyond the city walls, choosing the path of death. He goes to Olive Mountain. There, in the chill of the setting sun, Jesus approaches God His Father in prayer.

Let's pause our visual here—Jesus kneeling before the Father in a restless, unsettled prayer about the coming thorns of the cross.

Remember the apostle Paul's thorn in the flesh? You may recall that Paul asked God to remove his thorn. Not once but "three times."[5] Three times Paul pleaded with God. Then, after asking for the third time, Paul surrendered to God's ability to use his thorn as an opportunity, a gateway for good. Paul trusted that God could see more than he could see.

*If God said the thorn could be repurposed for good, then Paul believed it. Even if he couldn't see it.*

Now, in the evening dew of Gethsemane garden, we find Jesus, still physically healthy, anticipating the pain of the cross. Jesus, who created the thorn-free Garden of Eden, now asks the Father if He can avoid the thorns of the cross. Like Paul the apostle, who would later follow Him, Jesus will ask not once or twice. Three times He pleads to escape from His pain.

We can look in on Jesus as He prays these prayers. We see Him. The flesh of His back not yet notched by the shredding teeth of the Roman whip. The calloused flesh of His hands and feet do not yet have gaping punctures torn by the stakes that will drive through the tissue that holds His finger and toes together.

The skin on His forehead is sweaty as He agonizes. Is that perspiration, or is it drops of blood glistening in the dark? Jesus' moist brow does not yet bear the swollen trace of thorns that will push through the muscle and nerves before scraping against the white bone of skull.

Jesus, in this moment, has no thorns in His flesh. But He knows they are coming.

From the common thornbushes of the region, His thorns will be tied like barbed wire into a mock crown, puncturing the sensitive nerves of His forehead, bludgeoning their way through blood vessels, delicate facial muscle, and tissue.

Jesus knows those thorns are coming. And being just as fully human as you and me, Jesus begs God the Father to remove those thorns from His near future. He begs to avoid such sufferings in His flesh, in His emotions, in His spirit.

*What is that, happening to Jesus as He prays?*

He chokes on the uncontrollable, rhythmic, heaving sobs of grief. Of agony. He cries out in such desperation that, as He stumbles in circles, He falls to the ground,[6] scraping His body, weighed down by the sorrow of His coming thorns so that He cannot even raise His head.

Moments earlier, Jesus had asked His closest friends to support Him in prayer. "My soul is overwhelmed with sorrow to the point of death," He told them, using every available word of His era to describe despair and emotional agony.[7]

Jesus is suffering through the most difficult time in His life—and how do His closest friends respond? They fall asleep.

Here is almighty God, alone.

Here is almighty God, abandoned by His closest friends.

Here is almighty God, crying.

Here is almighty God, agonizing.

Here is almighty God, shaking and sweating.

Here is almighty God, physically undone by overwhelming emotion.

(All of this, not because God is weak, but because Jesus willingly, voluntarily, limited His God-powers when He stepped down into our human form; see Philippians 2.)

We know of Jesus the Savior. Jesus the Healer. Jesus the Judge who will return to earth to winnow out evil, who will cast Satan into hell for eternity. These are all true of Jesus. Just as true, Isaiah the prophet tells us, is that Jesus is the "man of sorrows."

To carry our weakness, He volunteered to live *under* our weakness, as one "despised and rejected by men, a man of sorrows, and acquainted with grief; and as one from whom men hide their faces he was despised, and we esteemed him not."[8]

Do you know how it feels to be so disfigured that people turn their faces away from you, grimacing? Jesus does. Your saving God is "familiar with pain."[9] He does not look down from a distance, unconcerned or uncaring about your hurts.

Here in Gethsemane, as Jesus stumbles in circles, as He crawls on His knees, clawing toward the sky and crying to the heavens—Jesus, who cannot lie, whimpers, "My soul is overwhelmed with sorrow to the point of death."[10]

As Jesus cries in prayer, struggling in sorrow, falling to the ground, He begs God the Father to take away the thorns that will soon impale Him.

And, being spiritually one with God Himself, Jesus could have chosen to avoid those thorns.

He asks the Father, "Is there any other way?" Any other way to complete the Father's plan, to restore humanity back to God, to repurpose evil, to forgive all who seek God? Jesus asks two times: "If there is any other way, take this away from me."[11]

Then Jesus prays "the third time."[12] He asks God the Father one last time if somehow He can avoid the coming pain of His thorns in the flesh.

He asks. He listens.

And then He surrenders.

*If God the Father said the cross could be repurposed for good, then Jesus believed it.*

———

You may recall the story of my son in the emergency room. Him, suffering under medical tests that frightened him. Me, a loving father having to hold my son down into a situation that he only perceived as painful and frightening.

*How must God the Father, the source of love, compassion, and good, have felt as He encouraged His perfect Son into the path of suffering—to redeem creation?*

Jesus, perfectly God, models for us the ideal life of a God-oriented human, expressing a trusting, childlike faith even while enduring the thorns of this fallen earth. Paul the apostle, as imperfect and sinful as we are, proves that sin-stained humans like ourselves can also trust the Father, as Jesus did, in our agony.

Jesus and Paul both trusted God the Father—more than they trusted themselves.

Jesus and Paul trusted God the Father—more than they trusted their pain.

Jesus and Paul trusted God the Father—more than they trusted their human emotion.

If God said there was a purpose, then they would believe Him and endure any temporary pain for the eternal glory that would follow.

Paul so believed this that he wrote, "I consider that our present sufferings are not worth comparing with the glory that will be revealed in us."[13] He says that on our journey through a broken, Rocky Flats world, we followers of Christ "share in his sufferings in order that we may also share in his glory."[14]

Paul's thorn included the loss of his career, multiple beatings, shipwrecks, the loss of his esteem and position in his community, death threats, homelessness, the loss of all personal possessions, imprisonment—all on top of his chronic pain and spiritual "torment" from Satan.[15] All of this, Paul said, is worth it because of the glory that God the Father promises. And all of this is "not worth comparing with the glory that will be revealed in us."

That is faith. That is "emergency room" trust in the Father's plan.

Jesus believed the same: "For the joy set before him he endured the cross."[16]

Here's what Isaiah wrote:

> He was wounded because of
>   our rebellious deeds,
> crushed because of our sins;
> he endured punishment that made us well;
> because of his wounds we have been healed.[17]

Jesus, in His humanity, trusted God the Father more than He trusted His human feelings. He "humbled himself by becoming obedient to death—even death on a cross! Therefore God exalted him to the highest place and gave him the name that is above every name, that at the name of Jesus every knee should bow, in heaven and on earth and under the earth, and every tongue acknowledge that Jesus Christ is Lord, to the glory of God the Father."[18]

Few Christians ever reach this point of maturity. But this is the ultimate adulthood of our spiritual development. Or is it the ultimate childhood? When we really trust God the Father so much more than we trust ourselves. When we really choose *His* plan over our own. When we really want *His* desires more than our desires. When we reach the place, like Paul and Jesus, where we stop insisting that God heal our pain or still our storm. The place when, after agonizing honestly before God about it, we say, "Not my will, but yours be done."

It's a fraction of a moment we can seize, capture in the grip of our soul, when we fully believe: *I consider that my present sufferings are not worth comparing with the glory that will be revealed in me and in my fellow believers.*

Jesus said as much in these simple words: "Not my will, but yours be done."[19] The word we translate "will" means "desire." So Jesus was saying, there in Gethsemane:

- "Not my desire [which, humanly, is to avoid excruciating pain],

- but Your desire [which is to work greater, eternal good through limited, temporary suffering] be done."

Jesus had prayed this prayer before, we know. He had prayed it hundreds, if not thousands, of times.

We know this because the twelve disciples once asked Jesus the secret to His powerful prayers. Jesus answered with a very short, very nonreligious (at the time) prayer. It started:

> "Our Father in heaven, may
>   Your name be honored.
> Your kingdom come.
> Your will [*desire*] be done . . ."[20]

Jesus' model prayer, which is often called "The Lord's Prayer," anchors itself in a daily surrender that says, "Father God, today, let *Your desires* be done in our lives. Not *our* desires, but *Yours*."

It is one thing to say these words, as a familiar religious chant. It is another to actually, daily, say, "Father, do *Your* desires in my life today, not mine."

It is still another to pray that kind of surrender while a painful thorn gouges into your life. To say, "Father, You know my desire is for this hurt to go away *immediately*. I know the day is coming when You *will* take it away. But, Father, while I'm here on earth, today, let *Your* desires be done in my life. Not mine."

"Father, I trust You more than I trust myself."

## The Strength of Surrender

If you've ever stepped onto a train or subway, then you know the strength of surrender. Once those train doors close, you have surrendered yourself to the strength and direction of the train. Your movement on planet Earth is no longer under your control. Where you will end up is entirely determined by the train to which you have surrendered.

When you surrender to the power of something stronger, it can take you places you could never take yourself. Surrender to an airplane, and you can be on the other side of the world in a matter of hours. We all surrender daily to various forces at work in our lives.

The strength of surrender depends entirely on the force to which you surrender. Your strength can become, in your time of surrender, that of a 747 airliner, that of a Ford taxi cab, or that of an elevator, depending on which one you step into and to which you surrender.

In Gethsemane, we see Jesus, in His humanity, willingly surrendering to the strongest force in the universe, God the Father.

Paul, with his thorn in the flesh, also chose the strength of surrender when he chose to trust God's plan more than he trusted his own emotions, reason, or pain sensors.

We would not be talking about Paul or Jesus today or wouldn't even know who they were if they had not stepped into the strength of surrender, into a good Father with far bigger plans than any human imaginings.

In their surrender, they attached their lives to a power far greater than any human capacity. We can also step into the strength of surrender when we choose to trust the Father more than we trust ourselves.

When God said Paul's thorn could be repurposed for good, *Paul believed it.* Even if he couldn't see it.

When God said the cross could be repurposed for good, *Jesus believed it.* Even if, it meant unimaginable suffering in the moment.

Today, in your hurts, God tells you He can repurpose your pain for good. *Will you believe Him*—even if you cannot see it?

## Your Gethsemane

Do you have a Gethsemane pain in your life? Can you relate, at some level, to Jesus' agony there in the garden?

Your Gethsemane is that lowest point, that darkest dark, that most difficult difficulty, in your life. We will each, at some point, find ourselves in the heaving sorrow of our own Gethsemane.

So many turn away from God in that agony when they are just inches away from the greatest strength of their lives and eternities, the strength of surrender in Gethsemane. It is surrendering your most powerful pain to the most powerful Healer in the universe.

Gethsemane surrender says, "God, even if it *doesn't* get better immediately, I will cling to You. Even if it *doesn't* go my way, I will trust You. I willfully choose Your desire over my own—because I believe in You and Your kingdom more than I believe in myself. I trust You more than I trust myself."

I cannot pretend to know the pain of your Gethsemane. But Jesus knows the pain of your Gethsemane. He carried the weight of your Gethsemane around His neck. Under that weight, "he offered up prayers and petitions with fervent cries and tears to the one who could save him from death."[21]

As the "high priest" who connects us to God the Father, Jesus is able "to empathize with our weaknesses," because He "has been tempted in every way, just as we are—yet he did not sin."[22]

For some, Gethsemane comes with a phone call about a car accident. A spouse or child, ripped away from earth in one unexpected moment.

For others, Gethsemane is leukemia, ALS, COPD, or another body-devouring evil.

Maybe yours is a Gethsemane of regret. When you realize that with one altered choice, the entire trajectory of your life would have been happier, full of life and smiles and pleasures that are missing today.

Gethsemane surrender is believing that in the life to come, all the cavities and voids of our present suffering will be filled with good in Christ's presence. Gethsemane surrender stubbornly trusts God in a way that stops insisting on our own desires in the here and now.

Gethsemane surrender acknowledges, "Yes, my life would have been easier and better if these things had gone differently." It is knowingly accepting the temporary pain, as Christ knowingly accepted His.

*Gethsemane surrender is the moment when we stop insisting that God do it our way.*

It's normal to struggle, to stumble, toward such surrender. My personal journey toward such surrender has had more retreats—me scurrying back into self-dependence—than faith-filled advances. I tend to stumble toward this surrender, retreat, and then rouse myself to crawl back toward it.

Jesus was perfect and sinless, and yet we saw Him clawing at the sky, crawling around in emotional anguish, working His way toward surrender. We saw Him question God the Father's plan, not once or twice but three times, as He stumbled toward the strength of surrender.

Don't let your hesitation stop you or guilt you. So you're reluctant to surrender your deepest pain? That's normal in Gethsemane. When you struggle to surrender your Gethsemane, you stand with Jesus Himself, with Paul the apostle, with me, and with an ocean of brothers and sisters who all have come to a place of saying, "Okay, God, I will stop insisting that You take my pain away. I choose Your plan, not mine."

*But think of how free your life could be if you finally let go of that Gethsemane pain where you keep insisting that God do it your way. Aren't you tired of holding on to it?*

Now is the moment to say, "Father, I surrender. Even if it *never* gets better in this life, I trust that You are good. I trust that You see more than I do, that You have a good plan, an eternal plan.

"Lord, give me the heart of Christ to cry to you daily, 'Nevertheless, Father, not my desires, but Yours be done.'"

Will you cry this from your heart, as Jesus did?

Temporary suffering leads to eternal glory in the Father's good hands. Only place your sufferings there. Only open your grip.

"Nevertheless, Father, not my desires, but *Yours* be done."

# CHAPTER 15

# *Secret Strength*

———

If you look at the world, you'll be distressed.
If you look within, you'll be depressed.
If you look to Christ, you'll be at rest.
*Nazi concentration camp survivor Corrie ten Boom*

*"I know I can't change* the circumstances around me," he told me. "I just want to have peace."

I was privately counseling a friend as he endured the most difficult months of his life. His storm was an uncommon one—a national media firestorm. Thanks to the marvels of the Internet and social media's ability to foment a shame mob, untold scores of strangers were belittling and scrutinizing him, misjudging his motives, outright making up stories about who he was.

While all of this was going on socially, he personally watched years of his life's work unravel and disintegrate before him. (By the way, the next time a well-known person becomes the laughingstock of the nation, we who know hurt and pain might remind ourselves that, underneath the notoriety, such people are normal humans—kids on the playground who want to be liked, just like the rest of us.)

My friend sought inner comfort. At this point, he knew his peace would not come from external circumstances. He was wise enough to know better. He needed to build up some *internal* peace if he was going to weather this storm.

To learn this skill, we opened the Bible to a passage where

Paul, burdened with his thorn in the flesh, describes an invincible internal peace. He writes about a peace that transcends, or goes beyond, the situations we find ourselves in. A peace that has nothing to do with our surroundings or even our human emotions.

This peace does not pretend nothing is wrong. This peace does not plaster on a fake smile *outside* while collapsing *inside*.

Nor does this peace peddle the empty lie that "if you have enough faith, your storm will immediately go away."

And this peace within is not insensitive. Jesus carried this peace everywhere with Him. Yet at an emotional funeral, He didn't tell heartbroken mourners, "Stop your crying! Don't you have faith? I can raise this dead man to life!" Instead, we're told, "Jesus wept."[1] Even more, Jesus "was deeply moved in spirit and troubled."[2]

Although Jesus was minutes away from raising the dead man to life, still He wept. Why? Because He hadn't created this world for death. Jesus wept at the contamination and brokenness of this Rocky Flats world. When death, sickness, or difficulty come your way, you can be sure that God weeps with you also.

Jesus shows how spiritual and God-like it is to weep. To mourn. And yet, even through our tears, even in our grieving, heaven's supernatural peace is available to all who know the rescue plan, to all who know the Rescuer, to us who possess the indwelling Comforter and Advocate, the Holy Spirit.

Paul carried a "secret" strength that gave him internal peace even as he limped over the jagged edges of fallen earth. Paul had not absorbed an outward peace from circumstances. Rather, he exuded an unquenchable, bubbling spring of peace that rose up within him, a spring that continued producing peace, regardless of the outer circumstances.

That's why he could write, "We are hard pressed on every side, but not crushed; perplexed, but not in despair; persecuted, but not abandoned; struck down, but not destroyed."[3] And "we do not lose heart. Though outwardly we are wasting away, yet inwardly we are being renewed day by day."[4]

Paul's physical health was wasting away when he wrote those words. His thorn in the flesh wore on him. And then his circumstances deteriorated. He was running for his life, then publicly beaten, then imprisoned.

So how did the apostle respond when things got *even worse*? Did his internal peace evaporate under such pressure? Not at all. When circumstances spiraled even further downward, Paul wrote, "Rejoice in the Lord always. I will say it again, rejoice . . . Do not be anxious about anything, but in every situation, by prayer and petition, with thanksgiving, present your requests to God."[5]

Paul is not advising a fake-smile denial of life's difficulties. Instead, he's saying that after you have mourned your difficulty, then:

1. Redirect your mind to thank God for the eternal rescue that has "already" started.
2. Talk to God about your difficulties. Ask Him for specific provisions, trusting that He is "not yet" done with His rescue. Confidently request every bit of peace and joy you need to continue enduring and surrendering, knowing that He will deliver these sustaining gifts *in* your storm.

Does that sound too easy? As proof that it works, Paul does not write this claim from a heated or air-conditioned five-star hotel. He had no warm mug of coffee sitting next to his papyrus and pen quills. Paul writes about his invincible internal peace from an unheated, uncooled, muddy jail cell.

And with the boldness of someone who has experienced it, he *commands* all who will listen to rejoice in the Lord always, and in every situation, to give thanks to God and bring our requests to Him. (The command is not to be thankful for *the situation* but for *the Savior*.)

On the heels of that command, Paul writes the following, likely with heavy, crude, blacksmithed chains digging into the flesh of his ankles and wrists: "I have learned the secret of being content in any and every situation, whether well fed or hungry, whether living in plenty or in want."[6]

This is the inner peace we seek. A peace that doesn't rest on food or wealth, on applause or salary. "Have learned" is the engine driving Paul's statement. Paul didn't simply choose to rejoice in his suffering all in one day. He *learned* this skill over a period of time; he learned it the only way anyone can—by learning it during multiple storms. (We know Paul learned this over time, because the Greek verb tense behind "have learned" implies something learned over a stretch of time.)

Paul *learned* how to make the "rejoice choice" in prison and then during shipwreck at sea. Whether betrayed or abandoned. Whether hungry, broke, or running for his life. In all of it, Paul *learned* that he could always "rejoice in the Lord." He could rejoice in Christ's coming victory. Rejoice in His faithful presence. Rejoice in His daily provision. Rejoice that His indwelling Spirit carries and comforts us.

"In every situation," Paul writes, we really can rejoice like this by redirecting our thoughts and by bringing our requests to God with thanksgiving.

This is a skill you and I can learn!

We will scrape a few knees and shed many tears as we do. Any worthwhile skill takes time and practice to learn. And what could be more worthwhile than fostering invincible inner peace and joy *within* the storms of life?

Remember the friend I mentioned as this chapter began, the one enduring at the center of a national media firestorm? I watched this dear friend pursue such *internal* peace through Christ. And I remember, as I watched and prayed with that friend, telling him this one day:

"You know, I think it's fair to say, this is the hardest thing you'll ever go through in your life. Actually, as a follower of Christ, this is likely the hardest thing you'll ever endure in your whole eternity. Can I tell you something—from an objective, outside observer's view?

"*You're making it.* You are making it through the hardest year of life you will ever go through, in your eternity."

As you read this, those words may be true for you right now too.

One year after saying those words, I remember meeting with my friend again. He still carried wounds in his spirit. Consequences he didn't deserve were still spinning, swirling, and whipping around him. He still hurt. The storm had not disappeared, but it had dissipated. He had made it. He challenged himself to *learn* Paul's skillful focus on the deep hopes and promises of Christ. Moment by moment, he kept choosing to rejoice in and give thanks for God's eternal promises, for God's daily strength.

God sustained him daily. God gave him internal peace, one day at a time. And he emerged from that year a better man, a person of refined character and sensitivity.

Paul the apostle knew, as much as any of us, how life's circumstances can change. He had reached the very top and descended to the very bottom of human experience.

He dined with rulers, and he floated shipwrecked in icy waters.

He slept in palaces, and he slept in muddy jail cells.

He talked to thousands of people who applauded him, and he talked to thousands who picked up rocks and began hurling them at him to kill him.

He cried, and he bled.

He'd been honored as a spiritual father, and he'd been slandered, lied about, misrepresented.

He owned money in the bank, and he owned nothing but the worn clothes on his weary shoulders.

He enjoyed great health, and now, as he wrote these words, he was enduring the chronic pain of his thorn in the flesh.

Paul had been through all the ups and downs of life. Now, at his lowest low in life circumstances, he describes a "secret" to being content, no matter what:

> I have learned the secret of being content in any and every situation, whether well fed or hungry, whether living in plenty or in want. *I can do all things through Christ—the one who gives me strength.*[7]

Notice what Paul is *not* saying. He's not saying what most of us assume—that the "secret" to contentment is changing our circumstance to something more comfortable. The secret is *not* a promotion, a raise, or a positive pregnancy test. The secret is *not* a court judgment, a miracle cure, a supernatural healing, or any other positive turn in earthly circumstances.

Instead, to paraphrase the passage in Philippians, Paul says, "The secret to finding joy, peace, and contentment has nothing to do with your circumstances and everything to do with Christ's strength."

That's worth repeating.

*The secret to finding joy, peace, and contentment has nothing to do with your circumstances and everything to do with Christ's strength.*

We all build our hope on something. By nature and by encouragement from well-meaning people who love us, we are taught from childhood to build our hope on the shifting sands of circumstance.

Hope for a new job. Hope for a good report from the doctor. Hope for the bad to get better.

There's nothing wrong with a new job or a report that "you're cancer-free." But building our internal peace on such hopes sets us up for certain letdown and devastation.

Paul learned to lift his hope and move it away from the quicksand of circumstances. Paul instead planted his hope on the "already" of what Christ has done at the cross and on our certain arrival in heaven, where we will be healed from our thorns and freed from our prisons.

Scripture reads, "Even . . . young men stumble and fall; *but those who hope in the* LORD *will renew their strength.*"[8] Despite Paul's fatigue, we see his internal strength *renewed.* We see God's strength suspending him above his storms of hunger, imprisonment, slander, rejection, and tormenting physical pain.

Paul had learned what it is to "hope in the LORD." He learned, through practice, that just like hammering a tent stake into soil, so we can hammer our hope into something sturdy. Paul learned to hammer all his hope "in the LORD." This was his secret to invincible joy, untouched by downturns or life circumstances.

Paul hoped in the Lord when savage mobs rushed at him to kill him. He hoped in the Lord when churches he poured his life into questioned his motives. He hoped in the Lord as he struggled under daily pain. As Paul hoped in the Lord, he saw God supernaturally renew his strength.

You can see God supernaturally renew your strength, too, as you learn to hope in Him alone.

There are no exceptions to the following. If you build your peace and contentment on the shifting sands of earthly circumstances, then you will live a shifting, shaking life.

Build your hope on your children, and they will eventually move away or let you down.

Build your hope on your career, and you will eventually have to retire or slow down.

Build your hope on your health, and no matter how fit you are, your body will eventually break down and breathe its final breath of earth's polluted air.

Every one of our bodies will wear out, regardless of our resources or talents. As creatures living in such disposable tents, we set ourselves up for sure disappointment when we build our peace and contentment on the drifty sands of well-being, comfort, and circumstances. One way or another, your lungs will stop breathing in the next seventy-five years, or sooner. So will mine.

That's okay. We have a greater hope than our lungs! We have the One who breathed life into being, who breathed galaxies into being, who breathed *us* into being.

We can do better than hope in a cheap lie that we'll always have easy earthly circumstances. We can live more stable lives, more eternally secure lives. As Paul pounded his hope deeper and deeper into the bedrock of Christ, he grew a strong, deep-soul peace, a contentment that stood unshakable through the storms in his life.

You can learn the same inner peace. As you pound your faith deeper and deeper into the bedrock of Christ, you can grow the same strong, deep-soul peace that stands unshakable through life's storms.

## Paul's Secret to Being Content, No Matter the Circumstances:

> I have learned the secret of being content in any and every situation, whether well fed or hungry, whether living in plenty or in want. *I can do all things through Christ—the one who gives me strength.*[9]

Here's a practical way of pressing this truth into our lives: *The secret is to turn my focus away from ending the storm, to claim Christ's sustaining strength in the storm, and to fix my hope on His plan to someday calm all storms, including mine.*

You might read that sentence again, even aloud, if you're able to. It's a good one to write on a 3 x 5 card or put on your phone or computer screen. You can put it this way too:

> *The secret is to*
>> *stop fixating on my storm,*
>>> *start claiming Christ's strength in my storm,*
>>>> *continue trusting His plan to still all*
>>>>> *storms, including mine.*

We often do the opposite. We fixate and obsess on getting the storm to calm, on getting the pain to heal. It's only natural that we do this. Sadly though, the more we obsess about the storm, the bigger the storm looks. As a result, we lose perspective of the reality that all storms end eventually.

When we fixate on the storm, we forget that heaven's strength is "already" available to carry us above the clouds. We also lose sight of the reality that, no matter how bad the storm ever gets, God's rescue is "not yet" finished. And "he who began a good work in you will carry it on to completion until the day of Christ Jesus."[10]

Earth's jagged edges will scrape you on your way through Rocky Flats. You will bleed. You will ache. As you hold your wounds, remember, *This is the worst it will ever be for you.* And as you crawl across this thin crust over hell, God is "already" giving you strength. He is walking with you, sustaining you, until He carries you up, out of here, to your true home.

Our day for healing and pain-free living is coming. Until then, the secret in your situation is to stop feeding your desire to change the circumstance and start focusing on Christ's strength available to you *in* the circumstance. We often want to change the weakness, but God is changing us. He's offering us heaven's sustaining strength, if we will look away from the storm long enough to receive it.

This is a big step in our journey toward heaven. The moment we stop insisting that God calm the storms. The moment we start trusting Him to carry us above the clouds. The moment we surrender our Gethsemane pain. The moment we look for His comforting presence more than we look for our immediate healing.

As we struggle to learn that way of living, we begin seeing the power of the storm to work good in our lives. Land that never sees rain clouds rarely bears fruit, and that's just as true of human lives. The great contributions come from souls who have been saturated under the storms of life.

*Too many people grit their teeth and survive, but they never get to see good come from their thorns and storms because they never make this choice.*

It's a choice to hope in God more than we hope in our health, wealth, or circumstances.

It's a choice to trust in Him more than we trust in our situation, doctors, finances, or feelings.

It's a choice to hope in His unfolding, long-term rescue more than we hope for a short-term change.

Paul learned this lesson by flying straight into the storm clouds of his chronic, painful thorn in the flesh. Trusting, even as the wind beat against him, that God would keep His promise to repurpose the pain for good.

For the rest of Paul's life on earth, those storm clouds were still present beneath him. Paul's thorn did not leave him until *he left* this earth. Through it, Paul came to know God's power, as well as God's loving comfort, in ways he never could have if had he lived a life free of pain or difficulty.[11]

You may recall that when Paul asked God to remove his thorn

in the flesh, God made this promise: "My grace is going to be sufficient for you."[12] *In that moment*, and in thousands of moments after, Paul had to make a choice:

- believe what God promised—that heaven's grace will sustain and strengthen me *in* my pain

or

- believe the pain that shouts at me in my present difficulty

Paul could easily have believed in his pain more than he believed in his God. It's our nature to do so.

God gave Paul strength to do the opposite. While living daily with his pain, Paul chose to believe God, to trust that God would *save* him for eternity and also *sustain* him on earth. And finally, that God would work eternal good from Paul's temporary pain.

When this seems like an impossible choice, remind yourself that Paul learned this skill over a stretch of time. Paul's journey to this place of invincible internal peace included countless ups and downs. So will yours. Nobody else can choose for you. Only you can make the effort to move your eyes from your storm to your Savior. No one else can decide if you will claim the promise of grace to sustain and strengthen you in your prison.

The moment you *do* make that choice, you further open the delivery door—and through that opening, heaven's strength further flows into your life through your weakness.

Will you keep moving forward with me to learn this spiritual skill? No matter how many times we fall and skid to the ground, we can get back up. We can choose again.

I know I will never learn this skill perfectly, but I can choose to keep getting back up. I won't be perfect in my efforts, but I can be consistent. And that's all our God needs from us—a faith that gets back to its feet, and steps out again.

Will you step out with me to learn, over time, Paul's secret to invincible inner peace?

Will you ask God to teach you this supernatural skill?

As we make this choice, we experience heaven's "already" power at work in our "not yet healed" weaknesses.

## Chapter Postscript

When I first mapped the path of our journey together, I placed this chapter ("Secret Strength") among the first chapters. I did so because, in my life, this is one of the most *practical* spiritual skills in this book—dragging my eyesight away from my difficulties and onto the promises of God.

As I kept writing, though, I realized this spiritual skill can come off as glib. A pat on the back. A Christian cliché: "Just get your eyes off your problems, honey, and onto Jesus." Wink.

I have watched well-intentioned Christians inflict pain and shame on hurting souls by spouting simplistic statements like that. How does such advice encourage the grieving widow? The childless mother? The limbless amputee?

Here's the difference between Paul's secret strength and the strength of the person who glibly says, "Just get your eyes off your problems": First, Paul *knew* the sting of pain in his own life. Second, Paul preached that we only get our eyes off our problem by establishing a bedrock understanding of who God is, where pain comes from (Rocky Flats), how trustworthy Christ's redemption is, and how eternal our glory will be once our sufferings end.

Paul's secret strength isn't glib, because it's undergirded by Paul's theology, by his understanding of pain, sin, redemption, healing, and eternity in Christ.

In a similar way, our study of Jesus in Gethsemane (chapter 14) can be summarized as, "Well, just trust God. Surrender to Him."

Again, apart from Jesus' bedrock understanding of who God is, these are empty, hollow words.

But built on Jesus' theology, on His understanding of pain, sin, redemption, healing, and eternity—well, when this is the foundation, "surrender to the Father's plan" transforms from empty words to an expanding universe of meaning and strength.

Jesus chose to "surrender to the Father's plan" in Gethsemane, because He knew how that chapter of temporary pain fit into the eternal story of redemption.

As I reflected on this idea early in the writing process, I opted to plant these two chapters ("In Your Gethsemane" and "Secret Strength") here, deep into our journey. In the chapters leading up to these, I have done my imperfect best to build for you a foundational understanding of why God can be trusted, what it means to trust Him, and what hopes you have as His child.

Now that we know scripturally where pain sprouts from and what God is doing about it, now that we know some of the powerful hopes we possess on our journey home—undergirded by this foundation, we can begin surrendering as Jesus did. We can begin dragging our eyes away from the storm and toward the Savior, as Paul did.

Paul's secret strength *does* come down to a sort of mental focus, a choice to stop fixating on fixing his circumstances and to instead start focusing on the thick details of Christ's work—past, present, and future.

Perhaps you're thinking, *But my pain is so severe that it's just not that simple for me.*

I would never compare your pain and suffering to my own. But I would challenge you that, built on the proper foundation of who God is and the hope His Word gives, the choice to *begin learning* inner peace actually is one you can make, no matter your circumstance. That's an act of the will that has more to do with you than with your pain. It's a choice to believe that God is bigger than all difficulty. And God is even bigger than *your* suffering.

That must have been hard to believe for Corrie ten Boom. Enslaved in a Nazi concentration camp during World War II, Corrie watched multiple friends and relatives suffer unjustly and die. Face-to-face with evil incarnate, enduring external circumstances more difficult than we can imagine, Corrie continued *learning* invincible inner peace, thanks to her faith in Christ.

God sustained Corrie's earthly life—even as she witnessed unthinkable violence, starvation, abuse, and trauma. Of the invincible inner peace that sustained her soul, Corrie said, "If you look at the world, you'll be distressed. If you look within, you'll be depressed. If you look to Christ, you'll be at rest."

That sounds a lot like what Paul learned and experienced too. Corrie and Paul both have the suffering credentials to back their claims. This works! And Corrie summarizes Paul's teaching so well:

> *If you look at the world, you'll be distressed.*
> *If you look within, you'll be depressed.*
> *If you look to Christ, you'll be at rest.*

Depression, anxiety, grief, heartbreak, the fiery breath of hell on our feet—none of these can be resolved with a simple greeting card slogan, with a three-step plan, or with a simple "just get your eyes off your problem and onto Jesus."

And yet getting our eyes off the problem and onto Jesus *is* the solution when we drive our faith deeper and deeper into the marvel of who He is, and how expansive His unfolding rescue plan is. While it is indeed very difficult to get our eyes off our difficulties, *it is possible* for the believer in Christ.

If Corrie could mentally focus on Christ in a Nazi concentration camp, if Paul could drive his faith deeper into Christ from his prison of pain, then, with practice, *we can too*. With time, with a wealth of broader understanding about Christ's rescue, with practice, with effort and lots of failure, we can eventually grow to a place where we *do* set our hearts and minds on Christ and his salvage operation.

We know Paul was constantly working at this skill, because he writes about it, time and again, in his letters:

> Since, then, you have been raised with Christ, *set your hearts on things above*, where Christ is, seated at the right hand of God. *Set your minds on things above*, not on earthly things . . . When Christ, who is your life, appears, *then you also will appear with him in glory.*[13]

And again: "*So we fix our eyes not on what is seen*, but on what is unseen, since what is seen is temporary, but what is unseen is eternal . . . *We live by faith, not by sight.*"[14]

Plainly ask God to teach you this skill. You are not His first student, and He is a gracious, patient, helpful instructor. One day at a time, you can begin to experience the willful redirecting of your sight away from your storms and back toward your Savior's unfolding promises.

# CHAPTER 16

# Pain and Purpose

———

The best way to cheer yourself is to
try to cheer somebody else up.
*Mark Twain*

*In describing creative geniuses* like John Lennon, Shakespeare, and
Picasso, *New York Times* columnist David Brooks observes that
the most creative, productive individuals are often tortured internally. That is, they struggle to resolve great tensions in their lives.
From this inward clashing, this conflict, the greatest works of art
and literature emerge. "Sometimes it happens in one person, in
someone who contains contradictions and who works furiously to
resolve the tensions within," Brooks writes.[1]

What is true of art and the creative process is also true of our
spiritual effectiveness. We like to imagine that God could best use
us in a casual, problem-free, conflict-free scenario. But the reality
is that the greatest spiritual gains come from women and men in
the throes of struggle and difficulty.

Think of Christ's impact on world history, the two billion
people who now revere Him in the largest faith tradition of all
time. Without the cross of suffering, there would be no Christ in
world history, no redemption of humanity. No Christianity without the cross.

Think of the apostle Paul's writings in the New Testament, the
most printed and purchased book in world history by a long shot.

Two millennia later, on the other side of the world and among the wealthiest societies of history, Paul's words remain threaded into our language. ("Labor of love," "powers that be" and "fought the good fight" are just three phrases he coined.)[2] Without his thorn in the flesh, there would be no Paul the apostle and no New Testament or Christian history as we know it. No Western hospitals and universities as we know them—if not for the Christianity of Paul the tormented apostle.

The question, then, is this: *What good thing does God want to work from your pain and struggle?* What does He want to work in the lives of others? What things bigger than you yourself could result from your surrendered hurt?

You may or may not see the answer to that question in your lifetime. But what you can do with certainty is to begin trusting, believing, acting, and living like God has the capacity to repurpose your pain and conflict for bigger good than you can imagine.

When you surrender your pain, you obtain a guaranteed outcome—God working some great purpose through it.[3]

Think about this: *Your greatest contribution in life may result from your greatest pain or weakness, surrendered.*

That was the case for Joseph, for Paul, for Jesus, even for Shakespeare and Picasso.

Joni Eareckson Tada has encouraged millions with her words about suffering, pain, and faith. Had Joni not been paralyzed in a diving accident, she never would have had such a ministry.

Nick Vujicic was born without arms or legs. Such physical disability would have led many into a life of despair and depression. But with Christ working through him, Nick has become one of the most inspirational speakers in the world, appearing on *Oprah* and on network TV shows, constantly communicating a message of hope in Christ. Nick has influenced millions of people spiritually. His greatest contribution in life is his greatest difficulty, surrendered.

From my own sufferings (tiny shadows of suffering compared to the suffering of Joni and Nick) grew this book for you. My thorn isn't as severe as some, but it is real. And when surrendered, even my meager thorn becomes a channel of life and hope for others.

Sarah Young's devotional book, *Jesus Calling*, will be read by millions of people today, pointing them to the heart of Christ. Young's books, which have taken up residence on *The New York Times* bestseller list, consistently outsell celebrity biographies and heavily promoted new works. Meanwhile, Young doesn't do a bit of promotional work for her books. Why not? She is too physically ill. Some days, she has the strength only to write a few sentences. So that's all she does in a day, as an act of worship. And God repurposes her surrendered suffering to become an extraordinary contribution.

Young fits, in a spiritual sense, into a common pattern of history. Influential writers with physical illness include some of the best from our era: Laura Hillenbrand and Flannery O'Connor, for example. They join the great writers of history who were bedridden with sickness. Their debilitating illness keeps them inside, reading. And their illness results in their writing great works of literature.

Without the cross, there is no resurrection.

Without sufferings in our lives, there would be no miracles.

Without our thorns and pains, there is little to be redeemed, little to show how extravagantly God can repurpose pain into healing, death into life, winter into spring.

What if we began seeing our pain, not as something to be endured, but as something to be redeemed? What if we began seeing our deepest hurts, not as things to be immediately healed, but as things to be laid down for the healing of others? Trampled grapes of sweet vintage, producing sweet healing wine for others.

Paul transitioned into seeing his pain and suffering this way. He moved beyond enduring or surviving his pain. He moved far beyond fixating on the taking away of his pain. He grew into seeing his pain as *opportunity*. He saw his pain for what it was—a literal "once in a lifetime" opportunity to *join Christ* in surrendering a suffering so God can use it to heal others. To heal nations.

The more Paul surrendered his suffering like this, the more he saw God use his pain to do great things Paul never could have done without a thorn.

It was a foretaste, an appetizer, of heaven's power to repurpose and redeem. And Paul got drunk on that "power through suffering surrendered." Looking back on his life and accomplishments before his thorn in the flesh, Paul writes that "whatever were gains to me I now consider loss . . . What is more, I consider everything a loss because of the surpassing worth of knowing Christ Jesus my Lord, for whose sake I have lost all things."[4]

Paul gave up every other comfort and pleasure of life to get more of this power through pain surrendered. Paul got so addicted to heaven's power that he claimed he existed for one purpose: "to know Christ—yes, to know the *power* of his resurrection."[5]

And what, we may ask, comes with the power of Christ's resurrection? Paul answers: "participation in his sufferings, becoming like him in his death."[6]

Read Paul's combined statement. On the heels of saying how delighted he is to have given up everything to taste heaven's power, he writes, "I want to know Christ—yes, to know the power of his resurrection *and participation in his sufferings, becoming like him in his death.*"

Have we ever considered it something worth living for, something worth giving up temporary pleasures for, to *join Christ in His sufferings*, to participate in His sufferings? To join in offering up to God a cross, which He can turn into a resurrection?

Paul wrote about this in Romans 8:17. There he teaches that we are "co-heirs with Christ, *if indeed we share in his sufferings* in order that we may also share in his glory."

And in Philippians 1:29 as well: "For it has been granted [literally *gifted*] to you on behalf of Christ not only to believe in him, but also to suffer for him."

---

What does Paul mean to "share" in Christ's sufferings?[7] Can we go back in time and be nailed to the cross next to Jesus? What is Paul talking about?

To share in Christ's sufferings is to surrender our suffering so God can work good from it for His bigger story. We share in Christ's suffering when we move beyond merely enduring our suffering (a good first step) and grow into seeing a greater purpose in our suffering. To expand our view beyond our own pain. To believe with a severe faith that our pain will be repurposed for the saving and helping of others.

Christ did not merely endure His suffering. He chose it in self-sacrifice for the benefit of others. He sacrificed self in the Father's plan to rescue an entire creation ripped away from the heart of God.

We join in Christ's sufferings when as believers we surrender our hurts to be used by God in helping others. We do not get to pick our cross of pain. Nor do we get to pick how our pain will lead to resurrection. But we *do* get to pick whether or not we will surrender our cross of pain for heaven's purposes in the lives of others.

We join in Christ's sufferings when we stop seeing our pain as something to endure and begin seeing our pain as something to be repurposed for the glory of God and for the good of others.

I have a sister in Christ who runs an amazing ministry for cancer patients. Why does she run this ministry? Because she was diagnosed with cancer at age thirty-six and told she had no chance of beating it. Her greatest difficulty has become her greatest contribution, because she surrendered it to be used by God for redeeming.

Who can best minister to the parent who has lost a child? Perhaps another parent who thought life could not go on without his or her own child, but who has seen that, in Christ, life can go on. That parent who has learned to live with a longing for reunion with that lost child.

Who can best minister to the raw, wounded divorcée? Maybe a person who had her own soul torn apart in divorce and, in that hurt, found the comfort of God.

How might God use your thorn as you surrender it?

*Your greatest contribution in life may result from your greatest pain or weakness, surrendered.*

Jesus walked among us and carried our pain so He can relate to our struggles. He is not being fake or phony when He empathizes with our hurting. By walking among us, He both showed and paved the way to salvation.

As we follow Christ in this fallen world, we too will get its cancers. We will suffer through its sicknesses and devastation. Its car accidents and assaults. All of the fallout of sin rains on us who trust Christ, just as much as it rains on our unbelieving neighbors. And in the drenching, we relate to them. We feel their hurt. Our tears mingling with the tears of neighbors we might otherwise ignore. And in that downpour, we long for Christ's full restoration of this fallen world.

Each new suffering presents a new opportunity to join Christ in His sufferings, *surrendered.* A new opportunity to join up next to another hurting person and show them God's plan for healing,

His undying compassion. We gently, patiently, show Christ to the hurting as we relate to their hurting.

Out of flawless, picture-perfect lives, we could only speak empty, hollow words about hope, purpose, and meaning in the midst of suffering. Instead, from our gaping wounds, our unveiled sufferings, we can speak hope-filled words bursting with emotion and legitimacy.

(God did not sanitize the bloody recourse of our sin from a cosmic distance. He dove into the seething sewer of humanity Himself to lift us out. And now we who follow Christ—we do the same; with bloody hands and muddy feet, with tear-filled eyes, we follow a God who is Redeemer.)

"Find life in Jesus' promises," we can say in love. "In my own pains, I've seen them work."

We are able to say this because we *have* seen His promises work. And we daily depend on those promises to carry us along.

Your greatest power is the power of your pain, surrendered.

Your greatest accomplishment in life may be your greatest pain, surrendered.

# CHAPTER 17

# Finish Your Race

———

Father of all mercy! God of all healing counsel!
He comes alongside us when we go through
hard times, and before you know it, he brings
us alongside someone else who is going
through hard times so that we can be there
for that person just as God was there for us.

*2 Corinthians 1:3–5 MSG*

*In Victor Hugo's classic,* Les Misérables, the hero, Jean Valjean, experiences forgiveness and then spends a lifetime helping others. Toward the end of Valjean's life, his adopted daughter, Cosette, falls in love with a young man, Marius.

Valjean is along in years, close to the finish line of life, when Marius gets trapped in an armed barricade, fighting against the French army. Valjean sneaks into the battle zone, dodging lead bullets and cannon shots, risking his life in order to carry Marius out of the crossfire, literally saving Marius's life.

To save Marius's life and free him from certain death, Valjean must carry him through the ancient sewer tunnels carved beneath the streets of Paris. These tunnels are piled with human excrement, infested with rats, unthinkable disease, and smell. The rainwaters of Paris wash horse droppings and rotten food into this subterranean cesspool.

Like Christ, who left the comforts of heaven to step down into the spiritual cesspool of earth, Valjean sacrifices his own health and well-being to rescue Marius, carrying him on his shoulders, wading through the stink of the sewage.

In his lifetime, Valjean saved many lives, but this final act was his magnum opus, his life-defining achievement. In so doing, he not only saved the life of a young man, but he also ensured the protection and well-being of his daughter, Cosette.

And it cost Valjean his life within months.

After a lifetime marathon of redeeming others, Valjean mustered all of his love, all of his compassion, all of his integrity, to push himself across the finish line in a final act of selfless love.

That scene—Valjean toting Marius through the Parisian sewers—ranks among my favorite in all of literature because it so visualizes the sacrifices Christ made when He willingly stepped down into our pain and suffering in order to carry us to heaven.

From our human perspective, we tend to see our own personal experience as magnified. We see the rest of the world beyond us as smaller. Somehow Jesus lived differently. He lived with His eyes on a big, broken world and on an even bigger, unbroken God. He lived his days on earth with eyes fixed on a finish line that was much, much larger than personal experience—the Father's plan to redeem humanity.

Jesus saw Himself as One sent to earth to accomplish a mission—God's redemption plan. And so, to Jesus, His suffering was not some inconvenience. His suffering was part of the path that led to His finish line—God's glory and man's restoration.

After Gethsemane, Jesus threw all of His will, all of His weight, into lunging across the finish line—at the cross.

The more you and I see our own personal suffering for what it is—not an end or affliction, but the path of our marathon journey toward heaven—the more we can lunge ourselves forward, throwing all of our weight and will at the finish line.

The more I view life this way (for what it truly is), the more

Mariuses I find scattered along my own path of suffering. Souls placed strategically by God to be picked up and carried toward the rescue as part of God's bigger plan for redeeming humanity from evil.

As you choose in your deep inner being to throw your weight toward the finish line, to accomplish any purposes God has for your sufferings, then you will begin to find other sufferers in your life.

Our journey toward the finish line becomes one in which we increasingly see through the facade of a world where everyone is happy, healthy, not hurting. We begin to see the bruises and wounds on all of the souls around us. From Beverly Hills and Silicon Valley to Calcutta and Port-au-Prince, humans are hurting. Some simply hide it better than others.

Some look smart and stylish. Some look slummy and slutty. They all carry, if we could only see, the war wounds of hurting people in a jagged Rocky Flats world. They hunger for hope, for purpose, for healing.

In our lifetimes, we have a brief opportunity to comfort the hurting with the same comforts of heaven by which we ourselves have been comforted. We're given this great power of heaven, it turns out, not so we will fully absorb the power within ourselves. We're given this power so it can be channeled through us and then redirected to comfort others. We get God's great power, hope, and strength so we can use them in rescuing and helping others.

This is a purpose worth living for. And as we throw ourselves into it, we live like Christ, who came not to accomplish His own purposes on earth but to accomplish the Father's:

- to repurpose the pain of humankind
- to redeem what was broken
- to resurrect what was dead
- to re-create what was contaminated

In the chaos and turmoil of this war zone world, scores of souls wander around us, not knowing the way back to God. Unaware of the good news that His strength can fulfill their deepest needs. They are strangers to the hopes we have—that this world is not the end, that our difficulties here are the worst it will ever be for us, that our pains will be repurposed for unimagined good.

Jesus stepped down to earth to create and show the way back to God. Even nonbelievers have to admit that Jesus has succeeded in that mission. His way back to God has spread in two thousand years from 120 believers to more than two billion. Christianity is now the largest faith group in the world.

And yet God loves billions more—men and women still trapped in the contamination of the fallout without hope, without a future, without daily strength or internal encouragement.

We are not in Rocky Flats merely to survive.

We are not in Rocky Flats to build a little bit of heaven down here in the rubble.

Each day we awake in Rocky Flats is another day in which our Father has reasons, purposes, and plans for us to carry out in this broken world.

Jesus put it this way: "My food . . . is to do the desires of him who sent me and to finish his work."[1] When Jesus woke in the morning, before He listened to His stomach, He went and listened to His Father.

"Father, what do You have for Me to do today?"

And then Jesus went and did it. Wherever it took Him. *Whoever* it took Him to.

This was so much Jesus' way of life during His time in Rocky Flats that at the end of His life, in a sigh of human relief, Jesus said, "Father, I have finished the work You gave me to do."[2]

He prayed, again: "Father . . . I have brought you glory on earth by finishing the work you gave me to do."[3]

When you consider that Jesus saw all of His life as a grueling, self-sacrificing rescue mission, a long-distance run to the finish line of the cross, it adds another dimension to His final words: "It is finished."[4]

For Jesus, the work was finished. The job was finished. The hardest thing He would ever endure in eternity was finished.

And for us, as we throw ourselves into the path of suffering-surrendered, we move closer and closer to such a finish line. This is the closest we believers will ever be to hell. And then it will be finished.

I want to finish my work—before I'm sealed in a place free of pain and suffering. I want to finish my work of pointing as many people as possible to the rescuing arms of Jesus.

*What a relief that day will be when our journeys through pain and suffering are finished!*

The apostle Paul spoke, thought, and lived this same way. He compared his lifetime of telling others about Jesus to a race. A marathon. The most grueling effort of his eternity.

When you compare your first 180 years of eternity, or the first 1,200 years of your eternity, to the fifteen or forty years you have left on earth, well, the earthly years of suffering shrink down a bit. You begin to see that you have this short window of time in which to grab as many hurting people as possible and drag them toward the rescue. Lighting the way, explaining the route, proclaiming the hope for all who hurt, shouting the good news of escape.

No one else can share hope with the hurting people in your life like you can.

As Paul stumbled toward the finish line of his life, having been tormented for decades with his thorn in the flesh, having been slandered, beaten, hated, stripped naked, pelted with stones, jailed, and lied about, he wrote, "I am already being poured out like a drink offering, and the time for my departure is near. I have fought the good fight, I have finished the race, I have kept the faith."[5]

Jesus described this scene for believers who lunge forward toward the finish line: God will pick up the believer who fed on the hopes of heaven and say, "Well done, good and faithful servant! You have been faithful with a few things; I will put you in charge of many things. Come and share your master's happiness!"[6]

Christians who live with such focus on the finish line bring life, hope, and joy into their worlds, believing that every new day in Rocky Flats is another day to fulfill the Father's mission. A day to unveil the good news of escape to another trapped soul. A day to pick up and encourage another who has fallen down on the journey home.

The men and women who are most heaven-focused, those who are single-minded about the finish line, all have one thing in common—sufferings. Suffering rouses us from the lulling illusion that this world is home.

And among these impaled heroes, I have never met a man or woman who gave their all in this brief race for Jesus who ever regretted it.

These people approach the finish line of death without regrets. From well-known runners like Billy Graham and Corrie ten Boom to millions more who ran equally hard without human fame, I have seen time and time again that a life poured entirely into Jesus' work of rescuing the hurting is the most overflowing life. Such an emptied life becomes the most fulfilled life.

When Paul looked back on the years he had not run for Christ, he regretted his wasted time and effort. He called those years "loss" and "garbage."[7]

And then he writes, "But one thing I do: Forgetting what is behind and straining toward what is ahead, I press on toward the goal to win the prize for which God has called me heavenward in Christ Jesus."[8]

Like Paul, we all have regrets. But it's never too late to start running for the finish line. In just three years, Jesus impacted human history more than anyone else ever has in a lifetime. Think what Jesus could do with the years *you* still have ahead of you!

So many have run before us in such great faithfulness. Paul waits across your finish line (no thorn in his flesh now). Jesus waits on the other side of the tape. Abraham, Moses, the Christian ancestors in your spiritual and biological family trees—grandparents, siblings, children.

Scripture describes this great crowd as a mass of fans at a sporting event. They're watching, even though you, with sweat-filled eyes and burning legs, cannot see them. They're cheering you on, cheering your faithfulness under the straining weight you feel as you run your race in Rocky Flats.

> Therefore, since we are surrounded by such a great cloud of witnesses, let us throw off everything that hinders and the sin that so easily entangles. And let us run with perseverance the race marked out for us, fixing our eyes on Jesus, the pioneer and perfecter of faith. For the joy set before him he endured the cross.[9]

With all of the shame and suffering, Jesus endured the cross, knowing the suffering was temporary and the glory, eternal.

And then Paul writes, "Consider him who endured such opposition . . . so that you will not grow weary and lose heart."[10]

Let us then run with endurance the race set before us. Whether we limp. Whether we wheel. Whether we stumble forward. Like Paul, we will soon say, "I have finished the race."[11]

Some days helping other runners who have fallen along the way. Some days being dragged by others who love us. In every step, clinging to our unseen faith in the life to come.

Whether we lie in hospital beds, stepping forward in heart. Whether we crawl. Whether we sprint, lungs burning, legs pumping.

When you can only lean forward, then simply lean forward.

To the finish line.

# Looking for Other Travelers

—————

*I wrote this book because,* as I traveled the country for speaking engagements, I began meeting hurting people everywhere. A taxi cab driver with an alcoholic son. A middle-aged dad with a cancer diagnosis. A young woman whose parents of twenty years are divorcing. I wanted to give hope to these hurting people but often had only ten or fifteen minutes of time in my brief encounters.

This book is my best attempt to create a biblical, Christ-centered gift of hope, which we can pass along to anyone in pain or need. I wrote it so it can be given to any hurting person from any background.

I now pack my suitcase with copies before I travel. And I am always amazed at the hurting folks God brings my way, so I can hand-deliver to them this summary of heaven's hope.

Maybe God will use you, in a similar way, to pass along this gift to a hurting person on your path. I pray that you have tasted an appetizer of God's comfort, salvation, and strength, here. I hope you continue feasting on these hopes. And I hope you share the gift with another.

For your journey through Rocky Flats, as you keep walking by faith, I've provided a few more tools for the road in appendix 3.

When we finish our journey and cross that finish line, I hope you will come and say hello to me. When we awake in that pain-free future of ours. When we've finally arrived with Christ in our true home, please look for me there. I look forward to seeing *you* there.

More than you know, I look forward to seeing you there.

> Therefore, my spiritual siblings, you whom I love and long for, my joy and crown . . . stand firm in the Lord, dear friends!
>
> *Philippians 4:1, my paraphrase*

# The Strongest Sufferers

*God is not limited by your weakness.* And you don't have to be either. God doesn't have to work around your weakness or in spite of it to love you. He actually wants to work right *in* your weakness. As a matter of fact, God does some of His best work in the storms of human struggles. And when you let Him work in yours, you are going to experience His strength like never before.

If you will give God the Healer permission to touch your wounds, then in this journey He will transform them. More importantly, He will transform *you*. By the end of the journey, you may even understand the odd prayer of the apostle Paul: "For Christ's sake, I delight in weaknesses . . . *For when I am weak, then I am strong.*"[1]

Was Paul out of his mind? To delight in pain, rejection, and chronic sickness? It sounds like Paul had a few wires loose. But this apostle, still regarded as one of history's greats, had learned the skill of accessing God's strength through the opening of personal weakness.

Some think Paul's success as one of the most influential people in world history came from his strength. It actually came from his weakness, which became a delivery door, a sort of secret entrance, for God's strength. He put it this way: "I have learned the secret of being content in any and every situation, whether well fed or hungry, whether living in plenty or in want. I can do all this through him who gives me strength."[2]

Paul calls his weaknesses the "secret" to accessing the strength of heaven. Paul, and Joy Veron as well, aren't the only heroes who learned to access God's strength through the door of personal weakness. The spiritual superstars of history are all, after careful examination, people who lived with pain and suffering. Sufferers who learned the secret of accessing God's strength through the hidden door of weakness.

Martin Luther King Jr. credited his impact to "the teachings of the Nazarene" Jesus Christ, "who promised mercy to the merciful, who lifted the lowly, strengthened the weak . . . and made the captives free."[3]

Abraham Lincoln expressed his weakness and God's strength this way: "Without the assistance of the Divine Being . . . I cannot succeed. With that assistance, I cannot fail."[4]

Literary genius Flannery O'Connor battled the debilitating chronic illness of lupus, which claimed her life at age thirty-nine. O'Connor was so aware of her weakness and God's strength that she wrote, "My intellect is so limited, Lord, that I can only trust in You to preserve me as I should be . . . My mind is not strong."[5]

The great Hudson Taylor, who helped thousands and shaped history with his China Inland Mission, once said, "All God's giants have been weak [people], who did great things for God because they reckoned on His being with them."[6] One of Taylor's biographers writes, "As he looked at himself, Hudson Taylor saw nothing but weakness."[7]

In suffering and pain, these heroes knew the depths of their weakness. And in those depths, they discovered the limitless power of Almighty God.

This is the spiritual skill we seek to learn together: our weakness as the opening where God's strength invades our lives. We seek to experience weakness-made-strong. We want to know it the way the apostle Paul knew it, not as a religious fact, but as moment-by-moment energy. An energy that changes every struggle, every challenge, every fear, and every year of our lives.

# Favored Sufferers

———

*The myth of "problem-free Christianity"* is so prevalent in America today that some will look at our prison analogy and say, "Oh no, that's not right at all. Have enough faith, and you will be immediately freed from your prison."

Well, that was not the case for Jesus' original disciples. Most of those guys, who had faith to perform miracles alongside Jesus, lived or died in actual stone prisons.

Neither did the apostle Paul's faith lead to immediate deliverance for him. Remember, Paul wrote many of his New Testament letters from the prison of his "thorn in the flesh." Not only that, he wrote much of it while sitting in literal prisons, exactly like the kind we imagined. (Footnoted here are more than a dozen verses in which Paul describes his suffering.[1])

Where you and I can imagine our sufferings as medieval prisons, Paul needed only to open his eyes and see the gray walls of rock in front of him. Needed only to shuffle his feet to feel the chilly stone floor beneath his toes. Needed only to awaken to feel the aching hunger in his stomach or to hear the dripping of rain leaking into his jail cell.

Few people in Paul's day were chained in so many jails across such a wide swath of the ancient Near East.[2] Paul's exceptional faith in Christ did not typically break open the doors for him to walk out of his prison in beams of light like a spiritual action hero.

From one of these prisons, Paul describes a joy, peace, and

contentment unlike anything he had tasted back when he was a free, healthy, wealthy man who did not know Jesus.

And Paul wasn't the only spiritual giant who found God's strength and joy right in his prison. Many of heaven's choice servants spent months or years in prisons—and not because they had done anything wrong. Not because God was upset with them either.

Joseph, whom God used to save nations, spent thirteen years as an Egyptian prisoner and slave—*while* God was delighted with him.[3]

Zephaniah, God's chosen prophet, spent a good chunk of his life in a Babylonian prison (present-day Iraq).[4] The same goes for Jeremiah, who suffered rejection, slander, and loneliness, as well as literal imprisonment *while* doing exactly what God had asked him to do.[5] God even told him to expect the rejection.

Jesus' cousin John the Baptist was chosen by God to declare that Messiah had arrived. Jesus called John the Baptist the greatest person in the history of the world.[6] What a privilege! And then John spent the rest of his life imprisoned by Herod Antipas, who eventually beheaded John as a party favor for a niece.[7]

The apostle John spent lots of time in Roman prisons and jails.[8]

Many of the first Christians got arrested and thrown in jail, simply for believing in Jesus.[9] This practice continues today in parts of the Middle East, northern Africa, China, and other areas, where the idea of problem-free Christianity insults the most faithful believers of our day.

Peter was imprisoned again and again.[10]

Paul's singing friend Silas shared his jail cell.[11]

In the early years after Christ rose from the dead, it became so common for believers to get thrown into prison that the early church made it part of its culture to visit jailed Christians who couldn't make it to the Sunday gathering.[12]

These imprisonments meant the loss of all earthly possessions.

Believers "joyfully accepted the confiscation of [their] property, because [they] knew that [they] had better and lasting possessions."[13]

Jesus warned Christians in one church, "Do not be afraid of what you are about to suffer. I tell you, the devil will put some of you in prison to test you, and you will suffer persecution."[14]

Much like Napoleon Bonaparte, John the disciple was sentenced to live out his final years on a secluded prison island. From there, John wrote the final book of Scripture, Revelation.[15] (John the disciple is not the same person as John the Baptist.[16])

From introduction to conclusion, God's people in the Bible are persecuted and jailed. Imprisoned on earth, but anticipating their escape into a better land with God. In the first book of Scripture, Genesis, God's choice servant, Joseph, gets sold into slavery and then imprisoned. In the final book of Scripture, Revelation, Christ's "beloved disciple" gets sentenced to another prison.

Peppered between those bookends we read stories in which God *does* miraculously heal or instantly deliver from pain. God invites us to ask for such miracles in prayer even today. And I have seen Him perform those dramatic miracles. But if you're reading this book, then you, like me, have likely not yet had a miraculous healing from *your* pain or difficulty.

And we must face the reality that even the believers who did get miraculous healings (such as Lazarus, raised from the dead as described in John 11) still eventually died earthly deaths. They left this earth knowing that death is not an end for the believer but a beginning to a better life that actually *is* problem-free.

Scripture focuses on our certain rescue in the future, not on pain-free living now. (This can be a difficult concept for folks like us who live in an age of immediate gratification.) Sure, some of God's people were miraculously freed from their prisons. But the majority more closely followed the pattern of Paul, who prayed three times for relief and then lived the rest of his earthly life with a thorn impaling his flesh.

It's often the same today. While all believers will eventually be set free from the prisons of our thorns, rarely do we gain our immediate freedom. This is why it's called faith—a persistent belief that Jesus will break us out and that He will sustain us until the great escape. A faith that continues to believe, no matter what.

There are times when God immediately delivers from cancer, heals the marriage, calms the addiction. The point here is not to minimize these miracles. Jesus encourages us to pray with that faith—as Paul did. Three times Paul asked God to remove the thorn, knowing God could. God's answer was that Paul would have that difficulty in his life until he crossed the finish line into eternity.

Here is where we find real, sincere, genuine faith. Faith that God's plan will be best in the long run—even if His plan does not immediately break me out of my prison or deliver me from my pain.

It is a low-level faith that prays for immediate healing. (And we hear lot of Christian songs and teaching about this sort of faith.) It is a higher-level faith that endures and continues trusting God when His response is not immediate. This faith that endures and persists through difficulty is the sort of faith that God highlights as great faith in Hebrews 11.

It's the kind of faith that enables Joy Veron (chapter 1) to live each day in her wheelchair, but to say with all honesty that she senses God's presence and goodness as she never did before her accident. This is the kind of faith that enabled Paul to uncover supernatural strength and power—even with his tormenting thorn. This is the kind of faith that will bring the gifts of sustenance to you in your prison too.

Find comfort in this list of spiritual superheroes. Their sufferings declare:

- When you find yourself in a prison, you're not alone.
- When you find yourself in a prison, you're not unspiritual or lower-class in God's eyes.
- When you find yourself in a prison, you're not unloved by God.
- When you find yourself in a prison, it doesn't mean you sinned or are being judged.
- When you find yourself in a prison, it doesn't mean God is punishing you.
- When you find yourself in a prison, God has not forgotten you.
- When you find yourself in a prison, you can count yourself in the company of the greatest spiritual heroes of all time.
- When you find yourself in a prison, it's not because you don't have "enough faith" to believe and get out. The imprisoned Bible heroes were full of faith, a quality that God Himself praises in Hebrews 11. And notice that not a single one of the imprisoned people listed above was being punished by God.

So, if trusting Jesus does not get you out of jail free, then what does it get you?

Here are four things you can cling to as you trust Jesus in your prison:

1. You have a sure escape being planned to break you out of your prison and to take you into a better kingdom that actually is problem-free *forever*.
2. Like Paul, you can find more joy, peace, and contentment with Jesus in the middle of your prison than you ever had outside your prison without Jesus.

3. *Because of* your prison, you can experience God's power in your life as never before.

4. You have meaningful answers, daily strength, actual purpose, encouraging companionship, and many, many more gifts right here in your suffering.

We are hard pressed on every side,
but not crushed; perplexed, but not in
despair; persecuted, but not abandoned;
struck down, but not destroyed.
*2 Corinthians 4:8-9*

At age eighteen, Joni Eareckson Tada broke her spinal cord in a diving accident and became paralyzed from the shoulders down. She has lived the majority of her life in a wheelchair. From her wheelchair, she has found God's strength, joy, and comfort in ways that many able-bodied folks never do. Joni explains God's compassionate, caring love like this:

God, like a father, doesn't just give advice. He gives himself. He becomes the husband to the grieving widow (Isaiah 54:5). He becomes the comforter to the barren woman (Isaiah 54:1). He becomes the father of the orphaned (Psalm 10:14). He becomes the bridegroom to the single person (Isaiah 62:5). He is the healer to the sick (Exodus 15:26). He is the wonderful counselor to the confused and depressed (Isaiah 9:6).[17]

When God looked down from heaven and saw you suffering with your unique thorn, He went out of His way to sneak into your prison to offer help. He invited all our thorns to be impaled into Himself so we can have a future in a place where there are no thorns. Not a single hurt for anyone who has trusted Christ.

And today, He whispers good news to you in your prison of pain and disappointment. He assures you that a breakout plan is in the works. Your days in that prison are numbered.

While He works out the details of your escape, He smuggles in sustaining helps to you. Distant as Jesus of Nazareth may seem from the prison of your thorn, He Himself is the assuring Delivery Man who sneaks these gifts to you, sustaining you right in your prison. He is also the One plotting and fighting for your divine escape.

Where you need answers, He is "the way and the *truth* and the life."[18]

Where you need strength, He is "the *bread* of life."[19]

Where you need a glimpse of hope, He is "the *gate*."[20]

Where you need a Friend to carry the load and guide us, He is "the *good shepherd*."[21]

Where you feel lost in the dark, He is "the *light*."[22]

Because of His help in your prison, you will be able to say, with Paul, "When I am weak, then I am strong."[23]

# Tools for the Road

———

*I want to give you* a few more tools. Though I don't have enough pages to write chapters about each tool, I want to be sure to hand them to you before we part ways.

These are practical ways of anchoring yourself in the strengths we've been learning. Ways to build your life around the hopes of heaven, strength-giving companions on your journey home.

***Tool 1: Friends on the Journey.*** If this book has encouraged you, then you could ask a few friends to read it with you. At IAmStrongBook.com, you'll find free videos, questions, and other tools for you to use to discuss the ideas in this book with a few friends. Do you know someone who is hurting or confused right now? That may be the person you can invite to walk with you through these truths.

***Tool 2: An Imperfect, Well-Intentioned Guide.*** I would be honored to keep in touch with you. If you're on social media, I'd love to be your friend there:

Facebook.com/JohnSDickerson
Twitter.com/JohnSDickerson

If you want to hear occasional encouragements from me by email, then shoot an email to Friend@IAmStrongBook.com.

I promise I will not give or sell your email to anybody else. I also promise I will not harass you. But I would love to drop you occasional messages of hope, encouragement, and direction.

You'll also be the first to know about any videos and other tools to encourage you on your journey home.

**Tool 3: The Guidebook.** The Bible can be intimidating. Most copies are thick as dictionaries. And we've all had history professors or teachers talk about the Bible as if it's a foolish collection of fairy tales. If all that weren't enough, it can be difficult to understand. The life-giving hopes you have found in this book all find their origin in the Bible. Here are some I recommend:

- *The Life Application Study Bible*, New Living Translation
- *The Life Application Study Bible*, New International Version
- *The Message*, paraphrase of the Bible, by Eugene Peterson

Each of these has a table of contents at the beginning, listing sixty-six different "books" in the Bible. Roughly two-thirds of the way down, you will find the book of John in the New Testament. I recommend you start your Bible reading there. Another great place to start is the book of Psalms, which you'll find about half-way down the Contents list.

**Tool 4: The Purpose Driven Life *and the Chip Ingram app.*** When you pick up your own personal Bible, you might also consider getting one of my favorite books, *The Purpose Driven Life* by Rick Warren. If you're really serious about getting to know God more, about walking with Him, then *The Purpose Driven Life* will help you, one day at a time, to do just that. Rick's easy-to-read book will give you an overview of the most important truths about God, His heart, eternity, and His Word for you.

Also, in the iTunes App Store, you can search for and download the Chip Ingram app. This unlocks a library of teaching videos and audio messages that can enourage you every day.

**Tool 5: Fellow Travelers.** In our journey, we're fellow travelers making our way home. How would you like a little company for the road? I encourage you to seek out some fellow travelers—other women and men who also see the brokenness of this world, along with the newness of life available in Jesus. The best place to do this is in a good Bible-believing church.

There are some "churches" that are not actually about Jesus or His travelers. Places that will take your money, your dignity, and your independence. Do stay away from those places. Yet there are thousands of gatherings of fellow travelers that are genuine and Jesus-focused. Places that are not after your money or dignity. Places where travelers encourage each other, pick each other up, and help each other on the struggle toward home. And yes, most of these places also have the word *church* in their name.

Just because some restaurants are terrible, I do not boycott all restaurants. Instead, I read reviews and try to know where I'm eating. I have pretty good luck finding good food. It's the same with churches. I can't encourage you enough to connect with a church centered on the Bible and focused on Jesus and His free gifts of salvation, grace, love, and hope. The strength of fellow travelers is unlike any other. I, for one, would not be where I am in life if not for the help of other Christians in my church family who pick me up, encourage me, and cheer me along.

At its best, church is not just a place you go; it's a group you become part of. You have fellow travelers who get to know you, love you, laugh with you. And cry with you too. You have men and women who visit you in the hospital—and whom *you* visit when they are in the hospital. People who look out for you on the road. Connecting with such a group of believers will give you a strength of relationship, warmth, and companionship that is simply incomparable. Irreplaceable. Money cannot buy it.

# Acknowledgments

*Thank you to my parents*, Dr. Dan and Cheryl Dickerson, who taught me to live seeking a better land.

Thank you to the readers of my first book, *The Great Evangelical Recession*. Your many words of encouragement kept me believing that God might use me again to communicate eternal truths in an age of noise and emptiness.

Thank you, Joy Veron, for demonstrating undeniably in our lifetime that God's strength can blossom in our most impossible tragedies. Thank you to my fellow travelers at Cornerstone Church in Prescott. Together, we have seen God's power in and through our weaknesses.

Thank you, John Sloan, for injecting muscle and tendon into this manuscript. Thank you, Wes Yoder, for believing in me before others—and for continuing to do so. Thank you, David Morris, Dirk Buursma, and Zondervan, for inviting me to communicate God's compassion to a hurting world with the hope that many will find comfort and help in these pages.

Thank you, Chip Ingram, for befriending and mentoring a young leader.

Thank you, Darrell Bock, Paul Nyquist, Kevin Palau, Clovis Barnett, Darryl DelHousaye, Michael Perry, David Kinnaman, Mark Bailey, Stan Cedarleaf, Harv Smith, Dan Rydberg, Frank Langford, and so many others who encouraged a young kid to keep speaking and writing.

Thank you to my confidante, partner, and best friend, Melanie. Like Christ, you make this weakling strong.

# Notes

## Introduction: Hope for the Suffering

1. Matthew 11:28.
2. Matthew 11:29, emphasis added.
3. 1 Peter 1:3.
4. Isaiah 40:29.

## Chapter 1: Living Proof of Heaven's Strength

1. Psalm 34:18.
2. 2 Corinthians 12:10—the reason this book is titled *I Am Strong*.
3. Isaiah 40:29.
4. Genesis 50:20.

## Chapter 2: Thorns in Our Flesh

1. 2 Corinthians 12:7.
2. 2 Corinthians 12:9–10, emphasis added.
3. 2 Corinthians 12:7.
4. 2 Corinthians 12:8–9.
5. The purpose of this book is to comfort those in pain. If you're searching for an academic or more theologically intense explanation of God's nature and our suffering, I recommend Philip Yancey, *Where Is God When It Hurts?* (Grand Rapids: Zondervan, 1997); Timothy Keller, *Walking with God through Pain and Suffering* (New York: Dutton, 2013); Randy Alcorn, *If God Is Good* (Colorado Springs: Multnomah, 2009).
6. Matthew 3:17.
7. Billy Graham, "25 Wonderful Words," *Decision*, July/August, 2005, http://billygraham.org/decision-magazine/july-august-2005/25-wonderful-words/ (accessed May 20, 2015).

## Chapter 3: Prisons of Pain, Chambers of Strength

1. 2 Corinthians 7:4 MSG.

## Chapter 4: Children in the Universe

1. Jeremiah 29:11 NKJV.

## Chapter 5: The Key and the Hammer

1. 2 Corinthians 1:3–4.

## Chapter 6: When You Hurt

1. Acts 9:31.
2. John 16:7.
3. John Ortberg, "Easy Job or Easy Yoke," video clip, Catalyst Conference, October 28, 2013, www.christianitytoday.com/le/2013/october-online -only/john-ortberg-easy-job-or-easy-yoke.html (accessed May 28, 2015).
4. 2 Corinthians 4:16–18.
5. Ephesians 3:16.

## Chapter 7: A History of Earth's Weakness

1. See Genesis 1:28–30; 2:15.
2. See Genesis 3:6.
3. See Genesis 3:18–19.
4. "2015 World Hunger and Poverty Facts and Statistics," World Hunger Education Service, www.worldhunger.org/articles/Learn/world%20 hunger%20facts%202002.htm (accessed May 28, 2015).
5. "Infographic: World Water Crisis," UNICEF, www.unicefusa.org/ infographic-world-water-crisis (accessed May 28, 2015).
6. "Malaria: Fact Sheet N 94," World Health Organization, www.who.int/ mediacentre/factsheets/fs094/en/ (accessed May 28, 2015).
7. "Orphans," UNICEF, www.unicef.org/media/media_45279.html (accessed May 28, 2015).
8. In every sunrise and ocean coast, we see remnants of the way this once-perfect world used to be—before the contamination. We are living in the ruins of a once-glorious creation. Describing this, writer Francis Schaeffer called us humans and our world "glorious ruins."

## Chapter 8: Strength That Is Out of This World

1. "2010 Copiapó Mining Accident," Wikipedia, http://en.wikipedia.org/ wiki/2010_Copiap%C3%B3_mining_accident (accessed May 28, 2015).
2. Ibid.
3. See John 10:10.
4. John 18:36.
5. John 14:2–3.
6. John 11:25.
7. See 1 Timothy 2:4; Titus 2:11.
8. John 3:16.
9. See 1 Peter 2:24.
10. John 14:6.

11. Romans 3:23.
12. Oswald Chambers, *My Utmost for His Highest*, ed. James Reimann (Grand Rapids: Discovery House, 1992), August 21.
13. Romans 5:8.
14. Romans 10:9.
15. Romans 6:23.
16. Romans 10:13.
17. Luke 24:5.

## Chapter 9: Already/Not Yet Strength

1. Hebrews 2:8.
2. Paul David Tripp, *Dangerous Calling: Confronting the Unique Challenges of Pastoral Calling* (Wheaton, IL: Crossway, 2012), 223.
3. Revelation 21:1, 4.
4. 2 Peter 1:3.
5. John 16:33.
6. Isaiah 40:30–31.
7. On the cross, as Jesus died to atone for our sins, He declared, "It is finished" (John 19:30). The price has been paid for our redemption. In this sense, it is complete. In a practical sense, however, the fully paid redemption that Christ has purchased will not be realized in its completeness until He returns to this earth as "Prince of Peace" to set up His kingdom and be worshiped for eternity.
8. Oswald Chambers, *My Utmost for His Highest*, ed. James Reimann (Grand Rapids: Discovery House, 1992), April 14.
9. See Philippians 4:7.

## Chapter 10: Trading Limits for Limitless

1. 1 Peter 1:13 ESV.
2. 1 Peter 1:17.
3. 1 Peter 1:4.
4. 1 Peter 1:5.
5. 1 Peter 1:6.
6. See 1 Peter 1:7.
7. See 2 Corinthians 12:10.
8. 2 Corinthians 12:9.
9. See Hebrews 12:1.

## Chapter 11: Smiling through Tears

1. I am paraphrasing to put this in modern terms. The same goes for some of the details that follow in Joseph's story. For the official dialogue and details of this story, see Genesis 37–50.

2. Genesis 50:20 ESV.

3. 2 Corinthians 7:9 MSG.

4. 2 Corinthians 7:10 MSG

5. 2 Corinthians 7:11 MSG.

6. 1 Corinthians 2:9 NLT.

7. Romans 8:28.

8. Rick Warren, *The Purpose Driven Life*, expanded ed. (Grand Rapids: Zondervan, 2012), 194–95.

9. Ibid., 195.

10. See Genesis 43:30; 45:2, 14–15; 50:1, 17.

11. Genesis 45:5, 7.

12. Genesis 50:20.

## Chapter 12: Rescue from Above

1. Romans 8:18.

2. Romans 8:19–21.

3. Romans 8:22–23.

4. Zamperini's story is told in the *New York Times* bestselling book by Laura Hillenbrand titled *Unbroken: A World War II Story of Survival, Resilience, and Redemption* (New York: Random House, 2010). For the suffering Christian, this story can serve as an inspiring picture of our temporary struggle against evil and our certain, coming rescue from above.

5. John 10:10.

6. "And the devil, who deceived them, was thrown into the lake of burning sulfur" (Revelation 20:10).

7. John 14:19.

8. John 14:2–3.

9. John 14:27–30, emphasis added.

10. See John 15:18–25.

11. Revelation 12:12.

12. For additional biblical information about the Devil, I recommend Erwin Lutzer's book *The Serpent of Paradise* (Chicago: Moody, 1996).

13. Ephesians 2:2 ESV/NLT.

14. See 2 Corinthians 4:4; Romans 6:16–23.

15. See John 12:31; Revelation 20:10.

16. See Revelation 12:9.

17. See 2 Corinthians 4:4.

18. See 1 Peter 5:8.

19. See Luke 4:18.

20. See Matthew 24:30; Mark 13:26; Revelation 1:7.

21. Hebrews 2:14–15.

22. Hebrews 2:8.
23. Hebrews 10:23.
24. 2 Corinthians 1:8–9.
25. 2 Corinthians 1:10.
26. G. K. Chesterton, *Heretics* (Rockville, MD: Serenity, 2009), 62, 82.
27. Romans 8:23–25.
28. Romans 4:18.
29. Romans 12:12, emphasis added.
30. Romans 15:13, emphasis added.
31. 2 Corinthians 1:10, emphasis added.
32. Psalm 33:18, emphasis added.
33. Psalm 119:81, emphasis added.
34. Titus 2:11–14, emphasis added.
35. Hillenbrand, *Unbroken*, 306–7.
36. Ibid., 313.
37. Isaiah 40:5, 10.
38. Matthew 26:64.
39. 1 Thessalonians 1:9–10.
40. Revelation 1:7.
41. Revelation 1:8.
42. Isaiah 40:29–31.
43. Revelation 21:1–4, emphasis added.
44. Quoted in Philip Yancey, *Where Is God When It Hurts?* rev. ed. (1977; Grand Rapids: Zondervan, 1990), 139.
45. Isaiah 35:1–4.
46. C. S. Lewis, *The Weight of Glory and Other Addresses* (Grand Rapids: Eerdmans, 1949), 7.
47. Ibid., 10.
48. Ibid., 14.
49. John 16:20–22.

## Chapter 13: Traveling Songs

50. Psalm 46:1–3, emphasis added.
51. Eugene Peterson, *A Long Obedience in the Same Direction* (Downers Grove, IL: InterVarsity, 2000), 100.
52. Ibid., 25.
53. Ibid., 28.
54. Ibid., 167.
55. Ibid., 31–32.
56. Ibid., 57.
57. Peterson, *Long Obedience in the Same Direction*, 100.

58. John Bunyan, *The Pilgrim's Progress*, ed. Jesse Lyman Hurlbut (Philadelphia: Winston, 1909), 17.
59. Psalm 138:7, emphasis added.
60. Psalm 37:1–2, 4, 39–40, emphasis added.
61. Psalm 9:9, emphasis added.
62. Psalm 62:1–2, 5, 8, emphasis added.
63. Psalm 23:1–4 ESV, emphasis added.
64. Psalm 55:1–2, 4–5, 16–18, emphasis added.

## Chapter 14: In Your Gethsemane

1. Matthew 27:27–29.
2. Revelation 21:1.
3. Genesis 2:9.
4. Revelation 22:2.
5. 2 Corinthians 12:8.
6. See Matthew 26:39.
7. Matthew 26:38.
8. Isaiah 53:3 ESV.
9. Isaiah 53:3.
10. Mathew 26:38.
11. Paraphrased from Matthew 26:39; Luke 22:42.
12. Matthew 26:44.
13. Romans 8:18.
14. Romans 8:17.
15. 2 Corinthians 12:7.
16. Hebrews 12:2.
17. Isaiah 53:5 NET.
18. Philippians 2:8–11.
19. Luke 22:42.
20. Matthew 6:9–10, my paraphrase.
21. Hebrews 5:7.
22. Hebrews 4:15.

## Chapter 15: Secret Strength

1. John 11:35.
2. John 11:33.
3. 2 Corinthians 4:8–9.
4. 2 Corinthians 4:16.
5. Philippians 4:4, 6.
6. Philippians 4:12.
7. Philippians 4:12–13, emphasis added, my paraphrase.

8. Isaiah 40:30–31, emphasis added.
9. Philippians 4:12–13, emphasis added, my paraphrase.
10. Philippians 1:6.
11. See 2 Corinthians 12:10.
12. 2 Corinthians 12:9, my paraphrase.
13. Colossians 3:1–2, 4, emphasis added.
14. 2 Corinthians 4:18; 5:7, emphasis added.

## Chapter 16: Pain and Purpose

1. David Brooks, "The Creative Climate." *New York Times.* July 7, 2014, www.nytimes.com/2014/07/08/opinion/david-brooks-the-creative -climate.html?_r=0 (accessed June 5, 2015).
2. 1 Thessalonians 1:3 ESV; Romans 13:1 KJV; 2 Timothy 4:7.
3. See Romans 8:28; 1 Corinthians 2:9.
4. Philippians 3:7–8.
5. Philippians 3:10, emphasis added.
6. Philippians 3:10.
7. See also Colossians 1:24.

## Chapter 17: Finish Your Race

1. John 4:34, my paraphrase.
2. John 19:30, my paraphrase.
3. John 17:1, 4.
4. John 19:30.
5. 2 Timothy 4:6–7.
6. Matthew 25:23.
7. Philippians 3:7–8.
8. Philippians 3:13–14.
9. Hebrews 12:1–2.
10. Hebrews 12:3.
11. 2 Timothy 4:7.

## Appendix 1: The Strongest Sufferers

1. 2 Corinthians 12:10, emphasis added.
2. Philippians 4:12–13.
3. Martin Luther King Jr., "The Negro and the Constitution," in *The Papers of Martin Luther King, Jr.*, ed. Clayborne Carson (Berkeley: University of California Press, 1992), 111, http://okra.stanford.edu/ transcription/document_images/Vol01Scans/109_May1944_The% 20Negro%20and%20the%20Constitution.pdf (accessed June 8, 2015).

4. "Three Versions of Lincoln's Farewell Address," Abraham Lincoln Online, www.abrahamlincolnonline.org/lincoln/speeches/farewell3.htm (accessed June 8, 2015).

5. Quoted in Flannery O'Connor, "My Dear God: A Young Writer's Prayers," *New Yorker*, September 16, 2013, www.newyorker.com/magazine/2013/09/16/my-dear-god (accessed June 8, 2015).

6. Hudson Taylor, *Hudson Taylor's Choice Sayings: A Compilation from His Writings and Addresses* (London: China Inland Mission, n.d.), 49.

7. Warren Wiersbe, *10 People Every Christian Should Know* (Grand Rapids: Baker, 2011), 45.

## Appendix 2: Favored Sufferers

1. 1 Corinthians 4:11–13; 2 Corinthians 2:12–17; 4:8–9; 6:4–10; 11:23–28; 12:7; Galatians 4:12–16.

2. For the first few of about a dozen such references, see Acts 20:23; 23:18; 24:27; 25:14–27.

3. See Genesis 39:20.

4. See 2 Kings 25:18.

5. See Jeremiah 37:15.

6. See Luke 7:28.

7. See Matthew 4:12; 14:3.

8. See Acts 4:3.

9. See Acts 8:3.

10. See Acts 12:1–17.

11. See Acts 16:23–40.

12. See Hebrews 10:34; 13:3.

13. Hebrews 10:34.

14. Revelation 2:10.

15. See Revelation 1:9.

16. The disciple John walked with Jesus and was one of Jesus' three closest friends. In fact, he was known as "the disciple whom Jesus loved" (John 13:23).

17. Joni Eareckson Tada and Steven Estes, *When God Weeps: Why Our Sufferings Matter to the Almighty* (Grand Rapids: Zondervan, 1997), 125.

18. John 14:6, emphasis added.

19. John 6:35, emphasis added.

20. John 10:7, emphasis added.

21. John 10:11, emphasis added.

22. John 8:12, emphasis added.

23. 2 Corinthians 12:10.

# About the Author

An *author and speaker,* John S. Dickerson has written for *The New York Times, USA Today,* and CNN, among others. His previous book, *The Great Evangelical Recession,* assessed the health of the church in the United States. John's writing has earned dozens of honors, including one of the nation's highest, the Livingston Award for Young Journalists.

John serves as Teaching Pastor in Residence at Venture Christian Church in Los Gatos, California. He lives in Silicon Valley with his wife and children.

**For more information, visit JohnSDickerson.com**

Access free resources and discover
additional books by this author at:

**JohnSDickerson.com**

Be the first to know about John's next books by sending an email to Friend@IAmStrongBook.com. Write "subscribe" in the subject line.